Dear Jessie

"Vive la Cuisine"

All the best

At to best

A TABLE AT
The Fields

Delicious recipes from Colin McGurran

Contents

A Table At *The Fields*

First edition printed in 2015 in the UK.

ISBN: 978-0-9928981-6-8

Written by: Colin & Bex McGurran

Edited by: Rachel Heward, Phil Turner, Andy Waple

Photography by: Tim Green

Designed by: Paul Cocker

Printed by: Bell & Bain Ltd

PR: Helen Lewis

Contributors: Bryony Johnson, Slawek Mikolajczyk, Ryan Cook, Peter Garlick

me:ze
PUBLISHING

Published by Meze Publishing Limited
Unit 1 Beehive Works
Milton Street
Sheffield S3 7WL
Web: www.mezepublishing.co.uk
Tel: 0114 275 7709
Email: info@mezepublishing.co.uk

Thank You

First and foremost I would like to thank my wife, Bex, and my beautiful girls Olivia, Emily and Jessica. Their constant love and support in hard times is what keeps me going and makes me push harder. Bex has also overseen the majority of the text in this book for which I am ever grateful.

Thank you to my boys Slawek, Ryan and Pete for giving up their time to write the recipes, assist with the photoshoots and mostly to enjoy a beer at the end of the day! I probably don't say it enough but thank you for making me look good!

Thank you to our Business Development Manager, Bryony, for her unfaltering capacity to adhere to my every whim and request, with only a slight grumble to my face!

A very special thank you to Alan Smith for the use of his land and for his time and expertise in helping me learn so much in my mission to be self-sufficient. Without Alan, none of this would be possible and I am so thankful to him for all he has done and continues to do for us.

Thank you to the team of Winteringham Fields, past and present, for their hardwork, dedication and support over the years.

Finally, thank you to our customers who over the last 10 years have joined us on this great Winteringham Fields journey. The journey has been bumpy at times and without their continued support we certainly would not be here today. We look forward to seeing what the next 10 years and beyond brings our way.

Colin McGurran

Welcome to
Winteringham Fields

What is the use of a book, thought Alice,

without pictures or conversations?

Welcome to Winteringham Fields, a special place that is not only our business, but our home.

Here, we have a close relationship with our produce and take great pride in every single ingredient that is served; with this book, we hope to inspire you to get creative and get cooking with the same ethos in mind. It's all about using the supermarket less, using your local people more and having a go at growing your own vegetables, fruits and herbs, or, if you can, even rearing your own animals and poultry.

Getting to know the produce you use every day in the kitchen will encourage you to think about food in a very different way. You will begin to appreciate the bounties of nature and understand how we, as humans, are more than just consumers, but producers too.

Obviously not everyone has the means to reap a full harvest, but what you can't grow yourself we want to embolden you to try and source from as close by as possible. Get to know the guy next door who grows great vegetables. In doing this you'll not only gain great-tasting, healthy produce; you'll also form new relationships with people, leading to life-long friendships. This is certainly one development from our approach at Winteringham Fields that we were not anticipating, yet one that we cherish enormously.

Our philosophy also takes things back to basics, and revitalises the notion of seasonal cooking. Whilst this makes good sense anyway, it will also open up a wide variety of menus to experiment with, and by using the freshest ingredients you are sure to discover new delights of taste.

Most importantly, remember that cooking is not a test; it is one of life's most pleasurable skills. Follow our field-to-fork approach, get involved each step of the way and you will soon feel part of the land yourself. And don't worry if some of the recipes here appear too complex; try starting off by trying a few elements of the dishes, gaining inspiration from the flavour combinations or methods used.

And to make you feel better, we've probably never had friends around for dinner when something hasn't gone wrong… flat Yorkshires (Bex's fault) none crumbly crumble (Bex's fault) over-cooked lamb (Bex's fault). So in other words, always have a good side kick who you can blame stuff on!

It's not a bible, but a guide to a style of cooking that is enriching, exciting and above all, absolutely delicious! We hope you enjoy it as much as we do.

Colin & Bex McGurran

Bryony Johnson, sales and business development manager

I joined the Winteringham Fields family in February 2008 as a receptionist. Soon after this developed into events coordinator and the role of personal assistant was also added to my job title. No two days are ever the same here. I've been given the chance to forge a role that is incredibly busy, but also fulfilling, and I love every minute. I am so proud to have been a part of making Winteringham Fields the place it is today and to see Colin receive the recognition he deserves makes every hard day worthwhile.

I have to admit though that Colin and I did not get on initially… He thought that I was too outspoken and grumpy (I am) and I thought he was a bit arrogant and dismissive (he is!) but after about a year our bond clicked. I think it's pretty safe to say that no matter what I do with my life, I will always have jobs to do for Colin, something that I am secretly quite pleased about!

In 2012 my personal life took quite a big change and I decided I wanted to move to London and do something completely new. I couldn't have asked for more supportive friends, let alone employers, than Colin and Bex. Of course this made it all the more heart breaking to leave. Being in London was a great experience and whilst I loved living in the big smoke, I couldn't help missing my Winteringham Fields family. I soon realised that I had traded my awesome job for the most mind-numbing role imaginable, so much so that I relished Colin's weekly emails asking me to do stuff for him - see, eternal PA!

Nevertheless, it still came as quite a shock to get a call from Colin after being away for eight months to discuss a new role he was thinking of. I was blown away by the offer of Sales and Business Development Manager, and the excitement of it made it so appealing that I really couldn't turn it down.

And so after a year I came home, back to where I belong. I'm still finding my feet with this new role but with so much going on it's not hard to sell a place and people that I adore and so fully believe in.

As much as I am a part of Winteringham Fields and the McGurran family, they are a bigger part of me and I am so proud of all of our achievements. I can't wait to see what the future holds.

Bridgey Johnson

Head Chef Ryan Cook

Chef de partie Gareth Bartram

Ryan Cook, head chef at Winteringham Fields

My name is Ryan Cook; I am twenty-two and started working at Winteringham Fields when I was eighteen. It was my first full-time job as a chef and I applied unaware of the tasks, challenges and life lessons that I was going to learn through my four year journey. I started on the fish garnish section, which was where I found out just how little I knew – not just about cooking, but things like how to organise my section as well.

I was soon given my first life lesson from Colin, when he took me to a cooking demonstration in Lincolnshire. He taught me how to write a bullet proof job list, how to make sure my chef jackets came out of the washing machine perfectly white, and how to sweep the floor. And from the moment I woke up if I perfectly made my bed, perfectly ironed my chef's whites and perfectly swept the kitchen floor, then I would subconsciously be able to cook a perfect piece of fish.

In my time at Winteringham Fields I have pushed myself to be organised, and have tried to learn something new every day. I want to know not just to cook a carrot, but how to plant it, water it, pick it, wash it, trim it and then to cook it.

The people around me at Winteringham Fields have helped me through tough times and joined me in happy times. But the best thing about my job is that I always finish my day with a smile on my face.

Gareth Bartram, chef de partie

After eating on several occasions at the Fields at different times throughout my career, I knew that this was the place to be if I wanted to work locally. I am now working at Winteringham Fields, heading up the meat section.

I began my journey working with a local Cleethorpes butcher at the age of fifteen. To begin with I was washing pots, but this quickly moved on to working alongside the owner, where my butchery skills began to carve my career path.

After completing NVQ Level 3 in Kitchen and Larder at Grimsby College, my first job in a professional kitchen was at Gordon Ramsay's Boxwood Café in Knightsbridge, London during the summer of 2005. I was eighteen and it was my first opportunity to see first-hand the discipline and work ethic of a professional kitchen. I was very fortunate to have this opportunity at such a young age and I knew the skills I learnt there would go with me to each kitchen I would eventually work in. The buzz of a busy, lively and explosive kitchen in the capital was a valuable experience, and cemented the decision that a chef's life was for me.

Deciding to return to Lincolnshire was not an easy decision after the hustle and bustle of the big city. But finding a job in a local seaside hotel (The Kingsway Hotel, Cleethorpes), would be the next step in defining my own style. After two more years of being home it was time again to move on so I headed to Wiltshire to Jack's Bar and Restaurant in Corsham. This was my first experience in cooking a more modern style of cuisine that I had been craving. It is here that I was able to put my butchery skills to good use once again and I discovered the importance of fresh, local, seasonal ingredients, earning an AA rosette in the process. It was two more years before I decided to return home and settle down.

Back in Lincolnshire I became head chef at the age of twenty-five at the Comfy Duck Bistro, Oaklands Hall Hotel, Laceby, and after a challenging few years I earned another AA rosette. It was at this time that I paid another visit to the Fields, to celebrate my wife's birthday. We had a great experience and just happened to 'bump' into Colin, two months later I was offered the position I currently hold.

Restaurant Manager Xavier Brette

Xavier Brette, restaurant manager at Winteringham Fields

After completing my HND in Hospitality Management at the Hotel School of Mauritius and doing internships in a couple of luxury hotels in Mauritius, I started to travel to gain more experience in the hospitality industry.

My journey abroad started in a two Michelin star restaurant, part of Relais et Chateaux in the south of France, then I worked in other Relais et Chateaux properties in Dorset and the USA. I also spent a few years as restaurant and bar manager in a five star hotel in Guernsey. Before coming down to the charming Winteringham Fields, I spent three years at Restaurant Andrew Fairlie, the only two Michelin star restaurant in Scotland, where I did my Advanced WSET.

Coming to Winteringham Fields was a new experience and a new challenge. The service here is very friendly, relaxing but at the same time very professional. We strive to provide the best service whilst sharing our passion and knowledge to everyone who visits. It's a privilege to be part of the Winteringham Fields family and part of the journey this remarkable place is on.

Executive chef
Slawek Mikolajczyk

Slawek Mikolajczyk, executive chef at The Hope and Anchor

I've spent the last seven years rising through the ranks at Winteringham Fields moving up to head chef and then onto executive chef at our sister pub, The Hope and Anchor.

I spent four years developing my craft as a cook at the local catering collage in my native Poland, then at the age of eighteen I made the decision to move to the UK to visit my relatives and learn English.

I started off working in a care home as a second cook then moved to a local pub. Then my passion for cooking lead me to take the head chef position in a newly opened gastro-pub. After one year I decided to take a step back and develop my culinary skills.

I accepted a job as a commis chef and joined the Winteringham Fields family in 2008, then within two years was promoted to sous chef. In 2012 I was presented with the opportunity of running the kitchen and became head chef. During my time at Winteringham Fields I've had the privilege to travel and learn from the best chefs in the country, including Gordon Ramsay, Raymond Blanc, Simon Rogan, Marcus Wareing, Tom Kerridge, Daniel Clifford and many more.

Peter Garlick, head chef at The Hope and Anchor

I joined Winteringham Fields in early 2011, starting as a commis chef after leaving college. Colin has guided me and made me feel not only part of the Winteringham Fields family, but also the McGurran family. To now be able to help create the same great family with the Hope and Anchor is such an honour. I owe a lot to the time and effort Colin and Bex put in to me; they got me to where I am today. Surprisingly, at first I didn't like Winteringham Fields. I started to let myself drop, but Colin wouldn't let me; he picked me up and pushed me as hard as he could, turning me into the well-rounded chef and person that I am now. For that I will be forever grateful.

After rising through the ranks at Winteringham I decided to move to London and become a part of the rat race, which was not an easy decision. However it's one I'm glad to have made as it allowed me to appreciate what Colin has created, to realise that the key to a good unit is to be a family. So after a short time in London, Colin called me back to be the head chef of his new venture, the Hope and Anchor pub. I couldn't wait to return. I am personally very proud to be a part of everything that has happened over the years at Winteringham Fields, and it's great to see Colin get the recognition he truly deserves.

Head chef Peter Garlick

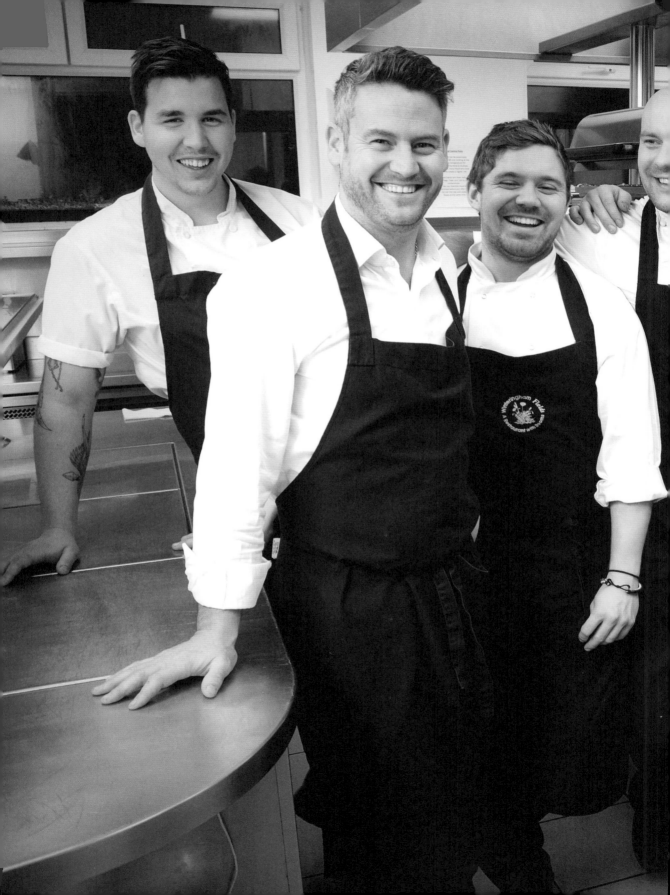

The history of
Winteringham Fields

"I can't go back to yesterday because
I was a different person then."

Who would have thought that in the shadow of a cement factory, on the banks of a murky river, boasting a name to make any sane person run in the opposite direction, our paradise could be found?

Here in the middle of nowhere on the south bank of the Humber estuary near the industrial steel town of Scunthorpe lies Winteringham Fields, a place that has transformed our lives.

I didn't know it was for sale the day I visited for lunch with my brother-in-law, but I fell in love with the place instantly, and I'll admit I did entertain the idea as I tucked into my food. There was something in its magnetism and charm that encapsulated me. A challenge, a risk and, realistically, a downright crazy venture - I wasn't without my doubts. Nevertheless I decided one day it had to be mine.

I found out soon after that it was for sale and my heart leapt to my throat. It was the opportunity of a lifetime. But logic was raining down on me; the trade had taught me some hard lessons and it's a daunting prospect taking someone else's hard work and attempting to turn it into something of your own.

So I went cold on the idea, but it remained there gnawing away at the back of my mind.

We were a young family at the time, and life in the catering industry had seen us endure more downs than ups. Our last venture, the 45-bedroomed Stoneleigh Hotel in Wakefield, was the epitome of Fawlty Towers when I bought it for a song. I thought I had been really clever, and would be able to turn it around. But it was a disaster from the start. The maintenance of the old building was horrendous and local people, who for long knew of its poor reputation, couldn't be persuaded that we were trying to make a difference. We ploughed cash into it and for three years it was money down the drain.

The whole episode was my worst nightmare but in a sense it was also the best thing that ever happened to me. When your back is against the wall you quickly have to learn how to be savvy, how to speak your mind, prioritise and develop a thick skin. Losing money is a sobering experience and while it makes you feel sick you become a lot more grounded and a lot less cocky.

It got to the point that one day, when I thought I was going to lose everything; I went out and bought a Labrador thinking he would be one thing the bank couldn't take from me if I went under. Perry is still with us today as a reminder of where we have come from.

Our luck did turn around and eventually the business started to make a profit, so we put it on the market straight away and it has since been converted into flats. That day I vowed never to buy a failing business again and set out to find something I could build up from scratch.

Winteringham Fields, in the heart of Lincolnshire, was hardly that. Run under the ownership of Chef Germain Schwab and his wife Annie, it was a hugely successful Michelin two-starred restaurant with a clientele coming from miles around. Far from being something I could build up from scratch, it was firmly established on the culinary map of England.

Yet my initial gut feeling had stuck in my mind and I knew I had to buy it when the opportunity arose. Looking back 10 years later I probably would not have done it today, but then, thankfully, I was young and naïve. Under the Schwabs it was a classic, traditional restaurant steeped in old-fashioned ways.

I had a grand plan and nothing was going to sway me – not even Bex, who initially was very much against the idea. "You aren't planning on moving us here are you?" was her immediate reaction. While I was being ruled by my heart, Bex was being sensible and was worried about the location. She thought I was making a mistake and was concerned how we could turn the place into something with our own stamp on it. We were both very young and inexperienced and she was due to give birth to our second child. The timing couldn't have been more inappropriate! But, determined to have my dream, we took the keys in August 2005.

To begin with we kept things simple, started off slow and copied their business model. Little changed until the recession of 2008 when trade slumped. Thinking it might be another Stoneleigh fiasco, we thought "here we go again" – but that experience had taught us not to panic. With level heads we set in motion a refurbishment, which also helped to introduce us to the community via tradespeople from the village and surrounding areas. We have since gone on to become firm friends with many of those who helped to build Winteringham to what it is today.

Further developments included the large room we added in 2007 to cater for groups and weddings. We also modernised and redecorated all of the lounges and bedrooms and ripped out the kitchen, starting from scratch to suit our own needs. On top of all of that we started redecorating and upgrading the guestrooms and terraces, built a new bar and bought Sussex House next door.

From Victorian style to modern country-living, we've introduced tartans, leathers, velvets and natural colours to soften the atmosphere into welcoming, comfortable surroundings.

In a nod to the past, we retained the Alice in Wonderland themed décor throughout the rabbit warren of the restaurant and bars, suiting the nooks and crannies of the place. Yorkshire artist Tina Antcliffe developed the Lewis Carroll theme by adorning the walls with drawings and quotes from the magical story.

In everything we have done we have tried to inject a sense of fun, aiming to make dining here a relaxed, enjoyable and attentive experience.

With the buildings and interiors up to scratch, it wasn't long before we started to apply our ethos and character to the menus. This involved plans to rear animals, plant vegetables and grow herbs in our own kitchen garden, but that's another story for another page…

Autumn

As the fields and leaves begin to turn golden our main root crops are getting ready to harvest. There is a wonderful variety of produce to explore and experiment with and everybody in the kitchen is excited. This season is all about the senses; colours, flavours, textures and even the smells are exaggerated, and you can gain a wealth of inspiration by simply taking a stroll down the lanes.

Provision for the colder months is vital, so Bex beds down the bees for the winter and the tup is introduced to the ewes in preparation for the lambing season in the New Year. Spring bedding plants are brought in December for overwintering in the polytunnels to ensure we have an early boost of colour in the spring.

Butternut squash velouté with chestnut cream

There are very few dishes out there that satisfy more than a simple warm velouté. This velouté depicts the ethos of Winteringham Fields as it is made using only one major product, our home grown butternut squash. We have the luxury of picking the butternut squash at the perfect ripeness to be enjoyed simply stewed down into this great autumnal warmer. Serves 4.

Ingredients

For the butternut velouté

500g butternut squash

50g unsalted butter

Salt

1g truffle oil

For the chestnut cream

200ml double cream

60g cooked chestnuts

½ tsp salt

For the pumpkin seeds

200g dried pumpkin seeds

50g sugar

For the butternut pieces

1 butternut squash

Salt and pepper, to season

Butter

Oil

Method

For the butternut velouté.

Peel the butternut squash and slice thinly.

Put all ingredients in a pan and cling film to steam until soft.

Blitz in a blender for 2 minutes then pass through a chinois.

To make the chestnut cream.

Whisk the cream until softly whipped.

Grate in the cooked chestnuts so very finely grated with the salt.

Continue to whisk until the mixture firms up and everything is fully combined, making sure you don't over whip.

For the pumpkin seeds.

Toast the pumpkin seeds in a pan.

Remove the seeds, add the sugar and then slowly melt in the pan.

As the sugar starts to caramelise, add the pumpkin seeds back in until they are all nicely covered.

Lay out across parchment paper to cool down, and then split up.

For the grilled butternut pieces.

Peel the butternut squash and slice to 1cm thick, square off each piece and cut 1cm strips one way, then 1cm the other way.

Season the pieces and cook under a grill with oil until they start to char.

Add a pinch of butter then turn over and repeat on the other side until nicely cooked.

Pork and salmon ravioli with pea velouté

☙☙☙

To me this dish sings harmony in its flavours; freshly juiced in season peas accompanied with smoked salmon and the richness from the pork works a treat. Freshness of ingredients is the key to this dish and the skill of making the pasta makes it all the more rewarding. Serves 4.

Ingredients

For the pork & salmon mix

500g pork trim (cooked and fatty)

250g smoked salmon

20ml pork or chicken stock

Pinch salt

Pinch pepper

For the pasta

1 whole egg

9 egg yolks

500g type OO flour

25ml olive oil

40ml water

For the pea velouté

1 bag frozen peas

Small bunch of mint

Pinch salt

For the shelled peas

1 bag frozen peas

For the pea powder

300g pea shells

3g mint leaves

For the smoked salmon oil

1 side smoked salmon skin

400ml vegetable oil

2 garlic cloves

Method

For the pork & salmon mix.

Chop the pork and smoked salmon roughly, but fairly fine and mix together in a bowl.

Heat up stock, pour into mix and combine well.

Add salt and pepper to taste.

Weigh into 18g portions and roll into a ball shape (tight and compact).

Place in the fridge to firm up.

For the pasta.

Place the flour in a bowl and make a well in the centre.

Slowly add the whole egg and yolks and mix together, incorporating a little at a time.

Add the olive oil and water in next and keep going for another 30 seconds.

Take out and knead until fully combined and smooth. Place in the fridge wrapped up to relax.

Roll out on the pasta machine to number 1 (slowly going down from 10), when at number 1 go through twice, or use a rolling pin and roll out as thin as possible.

Cut out 7.5cm round pieces and brush with a little bit of water to help two pieces stick.

Place the pork and salmon ball into the middle of one disc and cover with another piece. Push round to form a ravioli shape.

For the pea velouté.

Defrost the peas and then juice through a juicer with the mint.

Pass through a chinois and check consistency (add water if needed).

Season with salt to taste.

For the shelled peas.

Defrost the peas and shell into a tray over ice.

Save the pea shells for later.

Place shelled peas in the fridge until ready.

For the pea powder.

Dry the pea shells and mint leaves in the dehydrator, or place in a very low oven until completely dried out.

Blitz in a blender on high to form the powder.

Scrape through a chinois to remove any large bits.

For the smoked salmon oil.

Trim up the salmon skin into small pieces, put in a pan and cover with the oil.

Crush the garlic cloves and add to the pan.

Put on a very low heat to infuse everything for a couple of hours, then pass through a chinois.

Carrot juice

When you put something so simple in front of customers who are paying with their hard earned money, you have to be very confident with your product. Here we simply juice our own carrots that have been picked a few hours before the guests' consumption to resounding praise of guests' never having tasted anything so carroty!

Ingredients

Large bag of fresh carrots

Method

Wash and peel the carrots, ideally picked from your own garden.

Chop into manageable pieces for the juicer, then juice.

Pass all the juice through a chinois.

Place into a bottle and in the fridge.

When serving shake well, make sure it is ice cold and that the shot glass is fridge temperature.

Apple mint jelly

This apple mint jelly recipe comes from my mother-in-law.
We've tried to recreate it in the kitchen but to be honest we prefer it when she makes it.

Ingredients

1.5kg apples, chopped

1.3 litres water

1.3 litres malt vinegar

Bunch of fresh mint leaves

Sugar (for every ½ litre add 500g of sugar)

8-10 tbsp chopped mint

Method

In a large pan put the chopped apples, water and bunch of mint. Bring to the boil and simmer until the apples are soft, then add vinegar. Boil for another 10 minutes. Strain through a jelly bag overnight, or for however long it takes.

For every half litre of liquid add 500g of sugar. Heat and stir until the sugar has melted, then boil until jelly forms. Cool and add some chopped mint.

Bottle in sterilised jars.

Sweetcorn panna cotta

This dish was inspired by a fresh sweetcorn accompaniment to our neighbours' Swedish prawn salad. The combination is surprisingly fresh and very moreish. Very simple to achieve as well as a very rewarding eat that is perfect for a dinner party starter. Serves 8.

Ingredients

For the sweetcorn panna cotta mix

1½ litres sweetcorn, juiced

6½ gelatine leaves

For the prawn salad

600g king prawns

25g baby capers

1 tsp dill

130g mayonnaise

Pinch salt and pepper

For the cracker

200g plain flour

100ml lukewarm water

1 tsp salt

Maldon sea salt, to serve

Oil, to grill

Method

For the sweetcorn panna cotta mix.

Juice the sweetcorn from the tins including the liquid inside the tins, until you have 1.5 litres.

In cold water soak the gelatine leaves until soft.

Heat 150ml of the sweetcorn juice in a pan, to around 80°c. Squeeze out the gelatine and melt into the hot liquid.

Combine the sweetcorn mixes and whisk. Place into ramekins and leave in the fridge to set.

For the prawn salad.

Sprinkle the king prawns with salt and pepper and cook under the grill, or on a griddle pan.

Once cooked leave to cool and then chop through to make small rough pieces.

Place into a bowl then add the mayonnaise.

Chop up the dill and capers until they are a fine mix, add to the bowl and mix with a spoon.

Taste and season with a little salt and pepper.

For the cracker.

Mix all ingredients together in a bowl, once combined take out of the bowl onto a lightly floured side.

Knead for around 10 minutes until smooth, then cling film and put in the fridge for 2 hours to relax.

Roll out through a pasta machine until number one, when at number one go through twice, (keep flouring gently after it has been through the pasta machine to stop it sticking.

Cook under the grill, or on a griddle pan, with oil on both sides until completely golden brown and then sprinkle with Maldon sea salt.

Dry out on kitchen paper to remove the grease.

Nori crackers

Ingredients

For the Japanese sheet

1 pack Japanese wafer sheets
(or substitute for rice paper)

For the nori egg white

1 pack nori sheets
400g egg whites

For the prawn cracker

1 pack prawn crackers
Oil, for deep frying

For the caviar purée

1 pot caviar

For the garnish

Caviar purée
Dill sprigs
Nasturtium leaves
Nasturtium petals

Method

For the Japanese sheet.

Cling film the dehydrating trays.

Wet the trays all over one side with a little water.

Place three sheets down per cracker and slightly wet the top so they fully stick down. (this can also be done if you have an oven with humidity changing settings).

For the nori egg white.

Blitz the nori sheets to a powder in the blender.

Add the egg whites and blitz until fully combined.

Using a pastry brush spread an even layer onto the Japanese wafer sheets.

For the prawn crackers.

Blitz in a blender to get a crumb sort of size.

Put into a chinois and pass out the powdery bits.

Sprinkle over the nori wafers.

Finally, dry the trays in a dehydrator for 1 hour and 20 minutes on full, or place in a low oven until completely dry.

Once dried, deep fry at 180°c for 15-30 seconds, holding down with a spider so they do not curl up.

For the caviar purée.

Blitz on a low speed in a blender and slowly increase until it is fully combined.

Place in a piping bag.

To serve.

Dot the caviar purée around the cracker.

On the dots rest the petals, leaves and dill sprigs.

Caviar plates

Ingredients

For the soured cream

600ml double cream

3 whole lemons, juiced

15g dill, chopped

Salt, to taste

For the blini mix

30g fresh yeast

500ml whole milk

4 egg whites

400g buckwheat flour

For the caviar

15-20g Avruga Caviar

For the smoked salmon

18-20g smoked salmon

Method

For the soured cream.

Weigh out the cream and lemon juice into a bowl.

Whisk the cream until firm, but make sure not to over whip.

Pick the dill sprigs and finely chop. Then add to the cream and mix in gently.

Add a pinch of salt to taste.

For the blini mix.

Place the yeast, milk and flour in a mixer and whisk quickly until combined.

Place into a container with at least double the space of the mix, cling film and leave to prove.

Then place in the fridge until needed.

Whisk egg whites to a stiff peak and then fold in some of the blini mix, until all combined and the mixture has taken a darker colour.

Cook in a pan or under a grill, add plenty of oil and warm to a medium heat. Place a small round shaped amount of mix onto the oil, let puff up and firm, then flip and cook for around 1 minute on each side.

For the caviar.

Quenelle with 2 teaspoons.

For the smoked salmon.

Using long sliced smoked salmon, slice into inch thick strips.

Cut again into inch length pieces and overlap.

Roll up in rose shapes.

Tempura quail eggs

Ingredients

For the tempura batter

140g plain flour

14g baking powder

250ml sparkling water

For the quail eggs

1 pack quail eggs

Flour, for dusting

Method

For the tempura batter.

Mix together the flour and baking powder and slowly pour in the sparkling water whilst whisking.

Check the consistency of the batter. It should be thick enough to coat the eggs.

For the quail eggs.

Bring a pan of water to rapidly boiling with a vegetable basket inside.

Take the basket out and put the eggs inside the basket, then boil for 1 minute 55 seconds.

Put into ice water and leave to fully cool, then peel.

Roll in flour and shake off any excess, dip into the batter and then into the fryer for 30 seconds. This should give a crisp outside and a runny yolk.

Tomato gazpacho and garden salad

We made this tomato gazpacho for Red Nose Day on Great British Menu and it went down a storm.
Serves 4.

Ingredients

For the tomato gazpacho

250g plum tomatoes
1 tsp salt
1 garlic clove, grated
5ml vegetable oil
15g tomato purée
75ml tomato juice
1 tbsp icing sugar
7.5ml raspberry vinegar
100ml olive oil
Gelatine bloom, 6 leaves per litre
30g egg white powder

For the tomato skin gel

1 litre tomato juice
500ml tomato water
30g vege-gel (available in supermarkets)
1g agar agar
50g tomato purée
10 drops red food colouring
1g sea salt

For the fake tomatoes

Frozen tomato gazpacho
Tomato skin mix

For the olive soil

100g dried olives
100g muscavado sugar

For the horseradish cream

250ml double cream
1 lemon, juiced
3g sea salt
30g jar horseradish

For the garnish

Maldon sea salt
Pea shoots
Pea flowers
Mustard cress
Micro rocket cress

Method

For the tomato gazpacho.

Quarter the tomatoes.

Mix all the ingredients, except the gelatine, and bake in the oven for 1½ hours at 70°c.

Blitz all of the ingredients in a blender for 1 minute.

Chill for 24 hours and pass through a chinois.

Weigh the liquid and soak the right amount of gelatine leaves. (6 per litre).

In a pan, bring 200g of the gazpacho mix to the boil. Dissolve the gelatine in the mix then pour back into the rest of the gazpacho.

Chill until set.

Remove chilled mix from the fridge and whisk using an electric whisk until it has a mousse consistency.

Wrap each 35g portion in cling film tightly to create a tomato shape and then put in the freezer.

For the tomato skin gel.

Pass through a muslin cloth and leave to drip until no liquid is left.

Mix all ingredients together and bring to the boil.

For the fake tomatoes.

Unwrap the tomato gazpacho and dip into the hot tomato skin gel four times using a cocktail stick.

Place on a tray and remove the cocktail stick when ready, then place a real tomato stalk on top.

Leave to defrost and keep in the fridge for up to 24 hours.

For the olive soil.

Blitz both ingredients until rough powder.

Keep in a container until needed.

For the horseradish cream.

Mix all ingredients in a bowl.

Whisk until slightly under whipped.

Then into a piping bag for serving.

For the garnish.

Bunch theses herbs up and stick them into the cream so they stand up to create a garden.

Foie gras
and mushroom duxelles

This dish has been a regular on the menu at Winteringham Fields for some time now and it is such a pleasure to cook and even better to eat. We have evolved the concept over the years but have always stayed true to the complex nature of the eating. You have the luxurious fattiness of foie gras with your Amaretto jelly that melts on the tongue then paired with fragrant mushroom duxelle and finished with a light crispy Parmesan tuille that lifts all the flavours. Serves 4.

Ingredients

For the foie gras

1 lobe foie gras

For the amaretto jelly

500ml amaretto

300ml water

5 gelatine leaves

4g agar agar

For the Parmesan tart

150g Parmesan

Sprig of thyme

2 sheets feuilles de brick pastry

1 block clarified butter

For the baby onions

Silver skin baby onions

Vegetable Oil

Butter

Salt and pepper

For the Madeira syrup

300ml Madeira wine

25g sugar

For the mushroom duxelles

500g button mushrooms

100g banana shallots

50ml Madeira wine

50g dried mushrooms

2 garlic cloves

50ml mushroom stock

50g unsalted butter

Sprig of thyme

Pinch of fine sea salt

1 tsp lemon juice

Pinch pepper

Method

For the foie gras.
Portion into 40g pieces. Save any trim for foie gras parfait.

For the amaretto jelly.
Put the amaretto in a pan and flambé to burn off all the alcohol.
Once the flame goes out, take off the heat and add water. Leave to cool.
Soak the gelatine leaves in cold water.
When cool enough add the agar agar and the gelatine, and bring back to the boil whilst whisking.
Set into a small rectangle flat tray with acetate in the bottom.
When set, cut into 1 cm cubed pieces.

For the Parmesan tart.
Butter one pastry sheet with a pastry brush.
On the buttered side, grate with Parmesan all around.
Remove the thyme from the stalk, finely chop the leaves and sprinkle all around the Parmesan.
Butter the other sheet and place on top of the Parmesan sheet with the butter side facing into the middle, then press as flat as possible.
Set slightly in the fridge then cut out with a 7cm ring. Cook between parchment paper and 2 trays for 7 minutes at 180°c (until golden brown).

For the baby onions.
Halve all of the baby onions you need, 2 per portion.
Put a pan on the stove then add some oil and a sprinkle of salt and pepper. Place the onions in face down.
As they start to colour dark golden brown, add a little butter, then flip over and cook for 1 minute.
Take off the stove and leave to cool, then peel all of the skins off and make sure there are no roots on them.

For the Madeira syrup.
In a pan reduce the Madeira and the sugar until a syrupy consistency.
Place in a squeeze bottle.

For the mushroom duxelles.
Soak the dried mushrooms in 400g of cold water for around 1 hour (or until soft). Strain off the mushroom stock for later and wash the mushrooms under running water to remove grit.
Finely chop the shallots and garlic so they are almost minced (very fine), add in the thyme leaves picked from the stalks.
In a hot pan melt the butter and add minced shallots, thyme and garlic, sweat for 5 minutes without any colour.
Roughly chop the button mushrooms until small.
Add the mushroom stock and Madeira to the shallots, thyme and garlic. Reduce by half.
Finely chop the soaked mushrooms, put together with the button mushrooms and add to the pan.
Cook out most of the liquid with just a little left to hold the mixture together.
When almost finished, season with salt, pepper and lemon juice.

Leek, Parma ham
and Lincolnshire poacher

This dish truly represents the philosophy of Winteringham Fields; three major components, two of which are home grown being the leeks and the ham and the other is from a local supplier who shares our same philosophy. This dish is very well balanced and meant to be eaten as a salad.

Serves 8.

Ingredients

For the Lincolnshire kuzu

250g Lincolnshire poacher cheese, without rind

600ml milk

42g cornflour

For the hazelnut bread

(Makes 6 loaves)

800ml water

500g brown flour

1kg white flour

100g yeast

30g sugar

40g salt

300g hazelnuts

Method

For the Lincolnshire kuzu.

Grate the cheese into a pan then pour the milk over the cheese, bring to a low simmer for 10 minutes.

Pass through a chinois with muslin, making sure you squeeze all the liquid through.

Keep the whey in the chinois for later.

Pour your milk back into the same pan and add in the cornflour then put it back on the stove on a medium heat.

The milk will go quite thick after you add the cornflour and will continue to get thicker as you cook out the cornflour.

Keep whisking on a low heat for 5 minutes until the cornflour has fully cooked out.

Put in a plastic flexi mould or a flat tray and set in the fridge. If in a flat tray, when set cut out to shapes you would like.

For the hazelnut bread.

Place all the ingredients in a mixer making sure you keep the salt and the yeast separate and adding the water in last.

Mix on low for 5 minutes, then turn up to the next speed for another 5 minutes. Check the elasticity by pushing a finger to dent the dough and it should start to spring back and not be sticky. Then on to high speed for the final 5 minutes.

After this time place the dough in a large slightly oiled bowl, and put an oiled piece of plastic bag over the top. Leave to prove.

When proved, weigh out to 450g and roll for the bread tins.

Place the bread tins with the dough in a warm place, cover with a cloth to prove again.

When risen, cook at 210°c for 20 minutes.

Remove from the tins and cook at 180°c for a further 12 minutes.

Leave to cool then cling film and freeze. When frozen, slice thinly.

Place slices into half pipe tray and cook at 180°c for 5 minutes with a little oil to get a golden brown bread cracker. (Continued...)

Leek, Parma ham and Lincolnshire Poacher (continued)

Ingredients

Parma ham

For the leeks
1 leek

50g butter

Salt and pepper, to taste

For the truffle cheese
250g whey (from the kuzu)

2.5g salt

25g truffle paste

For the herb emulsion
20g tarragon

20g parsley

20g dill

20g basil

1 egg yolk

20ml white wine vinegar

300ml vegetable oil

Salt, to taste

Method

For the Parma ham.

Use wafer thin slices

For the leeks.

Wash and peel the first layer of the leek. Slice where the leek leaves split (this is where the soil will stop).

Season with salt and pepper and steam until soft.

Heat the butter in a pan, add the leek and roll round to coat. Then cool in the fridge until needed.

When cool, halve the leek lengthways, trim to the size you want, season the middles and cook flat down in a pan to char.

For the truffle cheese.

Mix together the truffle, salt and leftover whey.

Roll into a ballotine shape and freeze.

For the herb emulsion.

Pick all the leaves off the stalks of the herbs and blitz to a rough paste in a blender.

Add the vinegar and blitz slightly, then add the eggs and blitz for a few seconds again.

Slowly blitz and start to dribble the oil in. As it thickens, slowly turn up the power and keep drizzling the oil until it is all fully combined. It should be like a mayonnaise consistency.

Pass through a sieve, season with a little salt and then into a squeeze bottle or piping bag.

Grouse breast with textures of beetroot and olive soil

Serves 2.

Ingredients

1 grouse

Knob of butter

Sprig of thyme

1 garlic clove

For the olive soil

50g dried black olives

50g dark muscovado sugar

For the beetroot chutney

250g beetroot

25ml vegetable oil

35g shallots, chopped

1 tsp sherry vinegar

1 tsp horseradish

Salt and pepper, to taste

For the smoked beetroot

3 beetroots

Pinch salt

Hay

For the beetroot crisps

1 beetroot

Oil, for frying

For the beetroot gel

500g beetroot

25ml balsamic vinegar

Pinch of salt

6g agar agar

Method

Pluck the grouse until all of the feathers are removed.

Remove the legs at the hip joint making sure to cut the skin closer to the leg, so the skin fully covers the breast.

Cut from the point of the bottom of the breast through to the middle of the back to remove any intestines, making sure not to catch any of the breast.

Rinse and dry the bird.

Cook in a frying pan skin side down until golden brown, then on the crown. Add butter, thyme and garlic and baste the bird leaving some in the carcass to continue cooking.

Put in the oven for 4 minutes at 120°c.

Rest and cover with tin foil for 5 minutes, take off the breast and serve, or serve whole.

To make the olive soil.

Blitz both ingredients until you make a rough powder and they are combined together. Keep in a dry container until needed.

For the beetroot chutney.

Peel the beetroot and steam whole until soft.

Cool down, peel and grate.

Put the shallots and oil in the pan and fry until golden.

Add grated beetroot, vinegar and horseradish. Season with salt and pepper.

Serve hot, or cool and reheat later to serve.

For the smoked beetroot.

Wash beetroot and steam whole for around 30 minutes, until just soft.

Cool down then slice the beetroot around ½cm thick, then cut out with a ring cutter.

Lightly season all the cut out discs, put into a colander and cling film all around the top.

In a bowl light some hay and then cover with the colander. Cling film all around so no smoke escapes. Smoke for 15 minutes.

To make the beetroot crisps.

Wash beetroot and slice very thinly, deep fry at 190°c for 30 seconds and season, then serve.

For the beetroot gel.

Wash and peel the beetroot. Then juice the beetroot.

Mix all the ingredients in a pan and bring to the boil while whisking, then set in a tray at room temperature.

When fully set, blitz and then pass through a fine sieve and into a squeeze bottle, ready for serving.

John Dory and saffron lemon butter sauce

John Dory remains one of my favourite fish to eat. Its robust flavour works well with beach herbs and saffron as it can cope with other strong flavours without being overpowered. This dish represents the flavours of the beach with the fragrant lovage oil. Serves 4.

Ingredients

1 John Dory

For the lemon saffron sauce

200ml fish stock

200ml white wine

200ml cream

30g shallots

1 garlic clove

Pinch of saffron

1 tsp lemon juice

Caviar, to taste

40g unsalted butter, cold

For the sea vegetables

10g sea purslane

10g sea aster

10g samphire

Salt, to taste

For the lovage oil

100g lovage

200ml vegetable oil

Method

For the John Dory.

Take the four fillets off the John Dory, starting by going down the middle on the fat side and following the line of the bone until both fillets are off.

Turnover and repeat the process.

Then, skin the fillets.

For the lemon saffron sauce.

Finely chop the shallots and garlic and sweat a little in the pan.

Add the wine and reduce by a third, then add the stock and reduce by another third. Then add the cream and reduce by a third again.

Now add the saffron and infuse until you have a strong yellow colour.

Cube the cold butter up, put the sauce on a low heat start to whisk in the butter piece by piece, making sure the sauce does not start to boil.

Once the sauce has taken in all the butter and thickened slightly, add the lemon juice and a little caviar.

For the sea vegetables.

Pick down the sea vegetables so there are no dirty, woody or soggy bits.

Heat in a pan slowly with a little butter. Add some water to create an emulsion.

Season with a little salt and serve.

For the lovage oil.

Take the thick bottom of the stalks off the lovage and make sure you have 100g left.

Bring a pan of water to the boil add the leaves and then turn off and leave to blanch for 5 minutes.

Strain off through a chinois and dry on a J-cloth in a warm area.

During this time put the oil in a pan and heat to 70°c.

When the lovage is dry add both the oil and lovage to a blender and blitz.

Pass through a J-cloth into a bowl on top of ice so it cools quickly.

Rolled rack of lamb, lamb croquette and cabbage

Serves 8.

Ingredients

For the saddle

1 side of lamb, with fat on

For the aubergine

1 aubergine

1 garlic clove

Sprig of thyme

20ml vegetable oil

Pinch of cumin

1 tsp salt

Pinch black pepper

50g large spinach leaves, blanched

100g caul fat

For the lamb croquette

1 lamb shoulder

Herb salt, for the rub

Pepper, for the rub

1 onion

1 carrot

100g mushrooms

1 leek

2 celery stalks

Water/stock

15g cumin

Pinch salt

20ml lamb stock or lamb fat

Pinch pepper

Egg

Panko breadcrumbs

Flour

Oil for frying

Method

For the saddle.

Remove skin from saddle then remove the loin, keeping fat in one piece.

Clean loin, remove as much fat as possible from skin.

Using a hammer, bash the skin until it spreads.

For the aubergine.

Cut the aubergine in half and score the middle.

Finely slice the garlic clove and put into the middle of the aubergine, pick the thyme and add to the middle as well.

Add the oil, salt, pepper and cumin, push the aubergine halves back together and wrap in tin foil.

Cook at 180°c for 40 minutes.

Once out of the oven leave to cool then chop up until it is a fine mix. Taste to check seasoning.

Drain off the liquid from the mix using a chinois or sieve.

Lay the lamb skin flat on the side, placing the loin just off centre, leave a small gap and lay the fillets to the side.

Lay the large spinach leaves into the gap and against the loin and fillets.

Place the aubergine mix into the spinach evenly and roll the leaves over to cover.

Now roll all together with the skin so it is tight.

Roll the lamb tightly inside the caul fat and tie with string.

Colour under the grill (or on a griddle) slowly, to stop the caul fat ripping.

Place in the oven and cook at 100°c with temperature probe inside to 48°c.

Rest and cover with foil.

For the lamb croquette.

Rub the shoulder with the herb salt and pepper until nicely covered.

Colour evenly all over under the grill (or on a griddle).

Roughly chop all the vegetables for a mirepoix, and lightly cook in a deep tray in the oven to colour.

Place the coloured lamb shoulder onto the vegetables and cover with water or stock.

Cling film and then tin foil the tray. Cook at 160°c for 2 hours and then at 120°c for 1½ hours.

Take out of the tray and pick off the meat while hot.

Pull the meat roughly apart and add all of the seasoning.

Add the stock or fat and mix through until all is combined. Taste to check the seasoning.

Set on a flat tray with something pressing it to create a nice tight square shape.

Portion into 3x3 centimetre cubes. (Continued...)

Rolled rack of lamb, lamb croquette and cabbage (continued)

Ingredients

For the black garlic purée
50g black garlic

2 shallots

1 bulb garlic

Pinch salt

Pinch pepper

200ml cream

For the red cabbage gel
500ml red cabbage juice

50ml vegetable oil

25ml red wine vinegar

7g agar agar

Pinch fine sea salt

For the creamed cabbage
500g cabbage

100g carrots

50g white onion

50ml vegetable oil

50ml double cream

Pinch salt & pepper

For the cabbage leaves
1 savoy cabbage

Water and butter for emulsion

Pinch salt & pepper

For the cabbage hearts
1 savoy cabbage

Water and butter for emulsion

Pinch salt & pepper

Method

Whisk your eggs and set up three tubs, one for the eggs, one for flour and one for panko.

Coat in flour, shake off any excess in your hands, coat in egg drain off what is dripping, then roll in the panko.

Deep fry at 180°c for 30 seconds.

For the black garlic purée.
Peel the shallots and bulb of garlic, place into tin foil with the black garlic, salt and pepper and wrap tightly.

Cook in the oven for 1 hour at 180°c.

After it's finished in the oven, place into a pan and add the cream, then heat until all is warm.

Place all into a blender and blitz until smooth, then pass through a chinois.

Check seasoning and add more salt if needed.

For the red cabbage gel.
Juice a red cabbage into 500ml of juice, then mix with all the other ingredients in a pan.

Whisk together and place on a medium to high heat, boil the mix to cook out the agar agar.

Set onto a tray and leave until fully set.

When cool and set cut up and place into a blender blitz until smooth.

Pass through a chinois.

For the creamed cabbage.
Finely dice the onions and sweat with oil for 4 minutes.

Peel and grate the carrots and add to the onions, then sweat for 2 minutes.

Grate the cabbage and add to the pan and cook for 5 minutes. Make sure that none of the cabbage, carrots or onions are colouring by keeping it on a low heat.

Add the cream, salt and pepper to taste.

For the cabbage leaves.
Prepare and cut out the cabbage leaves into discs.

Wash and drain off the water.

Cook in a water and butter emulsion for 4 minutes, making sure the emulsion is seasoned.

For the cabbage hearts.
Prepare and cut out the cabbage hearts into triangle shapes (there should be a little bit of the green leaf on the outside).

Cook for 6 minutes in a butter and water emulsion, making sure your emulsion is seasoned.

Cook under the grill (or on a griddle) for 1 minute, until golden on each side.

Foie gras tarts

Makes 8-12 tarts.

Ingredients

For the tartlets

1 pack feuilles de brick pastry

1 butter, clarified

Poppy seeds

For the quince purée

2 quinces

150g sugar

300ml water

1 vanilla pod

For the foie gras parfait

250ml sweet white wine

250ml pear cider

75ml brandy

20g fine sea salt

1 bay leaf

Sprig of thyme

Sprig of rosemary

150g shallots, sliced

400g foie gras

400g chicken livers

7 eggs

800g unsalted butter

Method

For the tartlets.

Brush butter onto a layer of feuilles de brick then lay down so the butter is on the inside.

Sprinkle lightly with poppy seeds to ensure nicely covered and evenly spread.

Butter another piece of feuilles de brick and place on top of the other piece with the buttered side going onto the poppy seeds.

Place between parchment paper and in the fridge to set the butter.

Cut out and place into tart moulds with tart case and baking beans. Cook at 180°c for 5 minutes.

For the quince purée.

Halve and de-seed vanilla pod, place in a pan with the sugar and water and bring to the boil (to make stock syrup).

Place the quinces into a pan on a very low heat with the stock syrup and cook overnight at 80°c.

Peel the skin off and remove the middles (which are grainy). Then, blitz in a blender adding a little stock syrup if needed.

Pass through a muslin cloth to remove any bits.

Put into a piping bag or squeeze bottle for serving.

For the foie gras parfait.

Reduce all of the ingredients on a medium heat until it has the consistency of syrup.

Remove the herbs and vacuum pack the mixture.

Soak the chicken livers in milk overnight, wash and vacuum pack.

Chop foie gras and vacuum pack.

Vacuum pack the eggs.

Vacuum pack the butter.

Cook all of the vacuum packed ingredients for 20 minutes in a water bath at 50°c.

After 20 minutes, blitz the eggs and alcohol in a blender for 20 seconds on a high speed.

Add the foie gras and livers, then blitz for 10-15 seconds on a high speed.

Slowly add butter to create an emulsion.

Pass the mix through a chinois.

Place into a terrine mould or bread tin. This should make two.

Cling the top of the parfait pressed onto it, and cling over the container.

Cook in an oven tray with water, in the oven at 100°c with temperature probe in the middle at 57°c.

Cool in the fridge. Set for at least 6 hours. Transfer into a piping bag with a star nozzle.

Apple terrine and mock apple with walnut ice cream

Ingredients

For the apple terrine
20 cox apples
200g sugar
10g pectin NH (available online)
12g agar agar
20g butter

For the mock apple
300g Granny Smith apples
300ml apple juice
3 gelatine leaves
15g dried egg whites

For the mock apple dip
1 litre apple juice
50g vege-gel (available online)
3g agar agar
60 drops red food colouring
20 drops black cherry colouring

For the walnut ice cream
800ml whole milk
200ml double cream
200g egg yolks
200g sugar
400g toasted walnuts

For the crumble
250g butter
250g flour
250g sugar
187g ground almonds

For the Pernod gel
300ml water
100ml olive oil
90ml lemon juice
60g sugar
5 star anise
Sprig of thyme
2 tbsp Pernod
6g agar agar

For the garnish
Toasted walnuts
Sliced grapes
Sliced apples

Method

For the apple terrine.
Cut the apples into 8 and bake at 200°c for 10 minutes then leave to cool.
Brush another tray with melted butter.
Mix together the sugar, pectin NH and agar agar in a bowl, then scatter half across the bottom of the buttered tray. Pack the apples in really close together and sprinkle the other half over the top.
Cling film the tray and bake for 3 hours at 120°c.
Press and freeze. When required portion into long thick pieces.

For the mock apple.
Soak the gelatine in cold water.
Blitz apples and juice together in a blender.
Bring the apple mix to a simmer and add the gelatine leaves.
Add egg whites, place into the blender and blitz fast so all the powder has blended in.
Set into a square container in the fridge for 6-12 hours.
Whisk up until it starts to look pale and like a meringue.
Put into a plastic flexi-dome mould, smooth the top and freeze.
When frozen, rub 2 pieces on the side to loosen them up and then stick the halves together to create a ball shape. Place a small tooth pick in and freeze.
Weigh everything into a pan, whisk and bring to the boil.
Boil and whisk out for around 20-30 seconds.
Put into a square container and cool slightly.
Take out the apple balls with the tooth picks in, and dip into the mix around 3 times until they have a dark red colour.
Place onto tray and leave in the fridge to defrost.
Take out the tooth pick when defrosted and place in a chocolate shaped stalk.

For the walnut ice cream.
Toast the walnuts in the oven at 180°c until nicely toasted. Leave to cool then roughly blitz up or crush.
Infuse the walnuts for 30 minutes and then bring to the boil.
In a separate bowl, whisk the egg yolks and sugar until it is all combined and starts to go paler.
Heat the milk and cream until boiled, take off the stove for a few minutes and then pour a third into the yolks and sugar, then whisk very well so it does not scramble.
Pour the rest of the milk and cream in and whisk until all is combined.
Put back into the pan and cook out to 83°c.
Pass through a chinois and into an ice cream churner or a container in the freezer, whisking every hour to soften.

For the crumble.
Mix all the ingredients together in a mixer with a paddle attachment, until sandy in texture.
Cook at 180°c for 20 minutes, leave to cool and crumble up.
Store in a plastic sealable tub when cold.

For the Pernod gel.
Mix all ingredients together in a pan and bring to the boil while whisking.
Set onto a tray at room temperature. When set, take out all the star anise and thyme and then blitz in a blender.
Pass through a chinois and into a squeeze bottle.
Garnish with toasted walnuts, sliced grapes and slices of apple.

Chocolate tart and vanilla ice cream

Makes 8-12 tarts.

Ingredients

For the chocolate mix

300g dark chocolate

400ml double cream

200ml whole milk

2 eggs

For the pastry

300g unsalted butter

200g sugar

2 eggs

500g flour

For the vanilla ice cream

800ml whole milk

200ml double cream

200g egg yolks

200g sugar

5 vanilla pods

Method

For the chocolate mix.

Boil the cream in a pan. Add the chocolate to a bowl then pour over the boiled cream, mix with a spatula and then leave to cool slightly.

Beat the eggs with the milk and then whisk in the chocolate and cream mix.

Pass through a chinois to make sure there are no lumps.

Leave for when the tart case is ready.

For the pastry.

In a mixer with a paddle, beat the sugar and butter and then add the eggs and flour.

Make to the size you need (a large round mould is preferable) and line. Blind bake with baking paper and baking beans.

Leave to cool, then check for any holes or gaps and trim the top so nice and flat.

Preheat the oven to 200°c and pour the chocolate mix into the tart.

Place the tart in the oven, turn it off and time for 20-25 minutes, then check.

For the vanilla ice cream.

Cut down the middle of the vanilla pods and de-seed. In a pan add the milk and double cream, and then all of the vanilla pods and seeds.

Infuse for 30 minutes then bring to the boil.

In a separate bowl whisk the egg yolks and sugar until it is all combined and starts to go paler.

When the milk and cream has boiled, take off the stove for a few minutes and then pour a quarter of the mix into the yolks and sugar. Whisk very well so it does not scramble.

Pour the rest of the milk and cream in and whisk until all is combined.

Put back into the pan and cook out to 83°c.

Pass through a chinois into a container and freeze, whisking every hour to keep smooth. Alternatively pass into an ice cream churner.

If frozen in a container, whisk every hour until set.

Egg custard

I have fond memories of eating egg custard tarts as a child and so here I have tried to evoke memories of this. This is created by simply having warm soft custard mixture topped with nutmeg on a textured crumb base served with toasted pine nuts and raisins.

Serves 8.

Ingredients

For the sweet pastry

500g flour

300g soft butter

200g sugar

1 egg

For the custard

11 egg yolks

150g sugar

750ml cream

For the amaretto ice cream

150g sugar

150g egg yolks

600ml milk

400ml cream

1 vanilla pod

250ml amaretto

For the toasted pine nuts

Pine nuts

For the raisins

Raisins

Sauternes dessert wine

For the nut powder

10g cooked sablé (see page 158)

10g dry roasted nuts

Method

For the sweet pastry.

Mix the butter with sugar in a mixer using a paddle attachment.

Continually mix and add the eggs and then the flour.

Mix until all the ingredients have all come together.

Line into a square metal mould.

Cook at 180°c for 13 minutes until quite brown.

Cool down and then egg wash around the sides and bake for another couple of minutes to seal all the edges.

For the custard.

Whisk egg yolks and sugar together.

Boil the cream and once boiled pour over the eggs and whisk for 30 seconds

Pour egg mixture over the cooked pastry and cook in the oven at 100°c for 1 hour.

For the amaretto ice cream.

Whisk sugar and yolks together.

Boil milk and cream.

Scrape 1 vanilla pod into cream mix.

Once boiled, add amaretto and bring back to the boil.

Mix cream mixture with egg mixture and pour back into the pan.

Slowly bring to 83°c, then pass through a sieve and into an ice cream churner, or into the freezer and whisk every few hours to keep soft.

For the toasted pine nuts.

Roast in the oven at 180°c for 13 minutes.

For the raisins.

Soak in Sauternes dessert wine for 24 hours.

For the nut powder.

Blitz until you get a fine powder.

Macaroons

Ingredients

For the macaroons

300g icing sugar

300g ground almonds

2 x 110g egg whites

300 sugar, for syrup

30g sugar, for meringues

100ml water

2ml food colouring

For the peach ganache

1 peach, puréed

350g white chocolate

250ml double cream

20g gelatine

Method

For the macaroons.

Blitz the almonds and the icing sugar together in a blender until a very fine well combined powder, then put into a large bowl.

Make an Italian meringue; in a small pan make a syrup with 300g sugar and 100ml water. Bring to the boil and take to 110°c.

Whisk 110g egg whites like a meringue add the 30g of sugar, when the syrup is 110°c gently trickle into the meringue and keep whisking until cooled down.

Now mix in the next 110g egg whites with the almonds and icing sugar mix.

Fold in the Italian meringue in three separate parts using a spatula.

Put into a piping bag with a metal nozzle and pipe onto a non-stick mat or greaseproof oven tray to the size you need.

Let them dry for 20 minutes.

Cook at 140°c for 6 minutes, then after this time turn the tray and cook for another 6 minutes.

To make different colours add 2ml of food colouring to your meringue mix.

For the peach ganache.

Soak the gelatine in cold water.

Boil the cream and then pour over the chocolate, add the gelatine and then the purée and whisk together.

Set in the fridge in a container.

Put into a piping bag and pipe into the macaroon shells when ready.

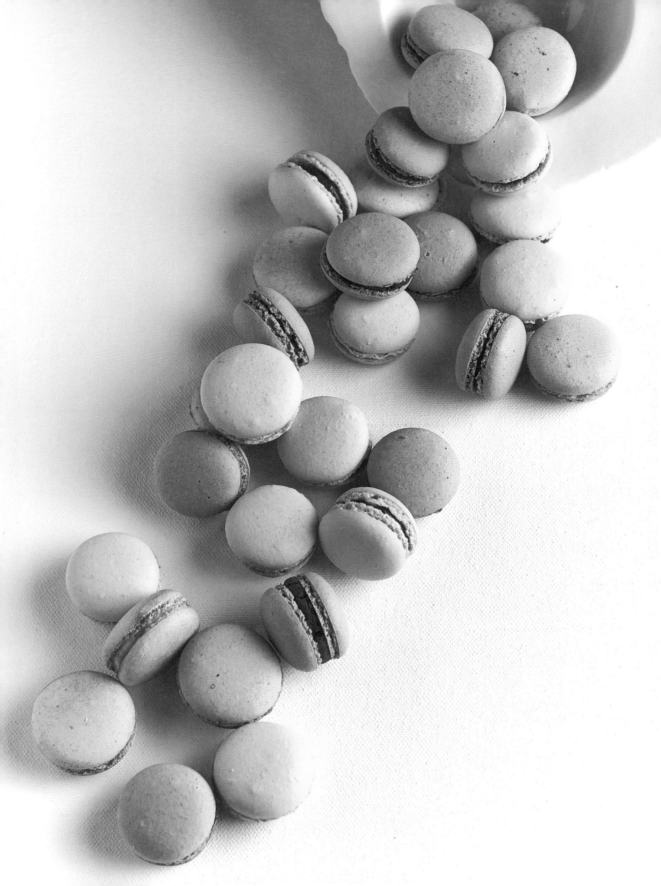

Colin on the set of the tv show, Great British Menu

(L-R) Chris Fearon, Alan Murchison, Phil Howard, Colin McGuran, Stephen Terry, Nathan Outlaw, Daniel Clifford, Simon Rogan

All About

Colin McGurran

"Who in the world am I?
Ah, that's the great puzzle."

As I was born in Zambia and spent my early years in Abu Dhabi, I suppose I had a fairly worldly introduction to different cuisines by the time my parents eventually settled in Bournemouth. This was where I attended the local catering college to develop my passion for cooking.

My first job in a kitchen was at Domaine des Haut de Loire in France: I hated it. An incredibly disciplined regime, its two Michelin stars were maintained through hard work and regimental discipline. Whilst I am impatient in the kitchen and get frustrated with the smallest things, that first job taught me to respect others around me. Rather than resorting to bullying I try to nail detail through precise organisation and forward planning.

Working in hotel management in Abu Dhabi after my time in the Loire Valley gave me a more rounded experience of the catering industry, which has helped me to keep calm under pressure on more than one occasion!

Bex came into my life in Canterbury as a student working part time in the café where I was front-of-house. At the tender age of 23, I bought The Woolpack Country Inn with my sister, a pub with a small restaurant in Yorkshire, and we moved north to run our first business together.

It went well from the start and I learned more about the ins-and-outs of the industry before we sold up for a profit to a brewery chain.

Following that came the infamous Stoneleigh Hotel. It was here that I learned how to deal with the trials and tribulations of disasters including everything from baths falling through ceilings to a groom running off with a bridesmaid… Like I said before, it felt like a real-life episode of Fawlty Towers at times, the dread of driving to work every morning wondering what could possibly have happened next.

Living and working at Winteringham provides a great work-life balance; the team have become firm family members. It's helped me to pursue other passions such as the Slow Food Movement, an organisation promoting organic produce, celebrating seasonality and doorstep shopping.

I believe we are too sanitised these days and supermarkets have stripped the fun out of shopping. I like the idea of shopping with the local butcher or baker, smelling the cheese from your local deli and picking through the vegetables in the grocery shop. It creates friendships within a community, enabling it to thrive, which for me, is what sharing and cooking food should be all about. We all need our supermarkets from time to time, but we also need to take the sometimes lengthy step of making the choice to buy certain things from our local shops. Make the choice the next time you are in your supermarket, put the sausages, milk and bread back, and stop in your local independent on your way home instead.

Colin giving a briefing on the service of his
Quail in the Woods dish at the 2012 final
Great British Menu banquet.

The ethos of
Winteringham Fields

"Yes, that's it!" said the Hatter with a sigh,
"It's always tea time."

The biggest change we have introduced at Winteringham Fields in our 10-year tenure is the implementation of my field-to-fork philosophy.

I'm a firm believer in using local produce. It's better for the environment, richer in flavour and makes good economic sense. So what better way to achieve this than by growing our own vegetables and herbs? And why stop there? Rearing our own animals and poultry would mean we would have complete control of the quality of care, making us absolutely certain that the meat in our dishes would be free range and superior in taste.

The spark of the idea was there, however the know-how was lacking. I hadn't a clue about growing anything before we came to Winteringham, so my goal as a chef was to source from the best suppliers from wherever they were.

When I was tucking into a full English breakfast one day, it struck me that everything on the plate could be produced right here in the village. I'd need chickens for eggs and pigs for sausages, bacon and black pudding. We already made our own bread and surely it wasn't too difficult to grow tomatoes. A homegrown Winteringham Fields full English breakfast... This led to a train of thought; I wondered what could be done with the rest of the pork from the pigs. I wanted to utilise every part of the animal and to do this, I'd have to get creative in the kitchen.

This was how our concept of field-to-fork was born. Our menus are now determined by our harvest and the animals we rear, which is the way it should be. We cannot rear enough meat to fully sustain the restaurant, but experiencing the aspects of hand-rearing animals is something that all members of the team enjoy.

Moreover, time in the fields has given us such a fantastic quality of life. The entire team's day is divided between tending to the fields and working in the kitchen. All of the brigade are prepared to get their wellies on and pull carrots. We're lucky to have a truly motivated team who are really passionate about cooking. I think this is because they really know from first-hand experience the full life cycle of the produce. You're less likely to waste food when you know the time and effort that's gone into producing it.

Some of the dishes on the tasting menu are 100 percent grown and reared by ourselves and we are averaging about 80 percent home production for vegetables, poultry, lamb and pork overall. Our fish producers and local farmers all contribute to our annual cycle, and this is the basis for our One Mile Menu.

Produce and *Planting*

"Of Cabbages and Kings ..."

One of the nice romantic things about the village of Winteringham is that the surrounding fields have names that date back centuries. We have the likes of Puddingpoke, Nanny Willey's Parlour, Whancho Field, Backside and Kettle Bottoms, to name a few (of the funniest). Starting with a few of Bex's pretty chickens it blossomed into the rearing of lambs and then pigs as well, bringing us into contact with local farmers who helped us to realise that we could do a lot more for ourselves.

Investing in a polytunnel meant we could grow salad crops, which went so successfully that we now we have three tunnels and have to employ a full time gardener, who grows micro herbs, tomatoes, salads, cucumbers, and mini water melons. Local farmer Alan Smith grows most of our vegetables for us in his fields. At the end of the summer we see courgettes, sweetcorn and leeks, and later our fabulous root and brassica crops – from kale, carrots, cauliflowers, broccoli, and turnips to simply superb swedes.

After four years we are largely self-sufficient for a good proportion of the year. On top of that, it has allowed us to experiment with crops; sometimes we grow them beyond their best to see what we can use the flower heads for.

The team goes to the fields twice a day to harvest, so the vegetables we're serving have often been picked no more than three hours previously.

And it's not just all about vegetables. Bex is growing pears, cherries, plums, apples and apricots, meaning the dessert menu doesn't miss out on the homegrown treatment. She also has five beehives, which are a learning curve and cause more stings than honey, but when she does produce honey we take full advantage in the kitchen.

Whilst this is undoubtedly an exciting, fun and rewarding way of life, it's also been a bit of an eye opener - to say the least! Prior to this I hadn't a clue about growing vegetables, and as you can imagine rearing animals can be a bit traumatic at times, especially when it is round up time and you end up muddier than the pigs! We also lost all of the chickens last year to foxes. Bex was devastated as Bryony had bought her four Lincolnshire Buffs for her birthday, and they had succumbed to Mr Fox first… I suppose this is the life of a farmer but it was a shock to the system to begin with!

Winter

The village is cold, grey and misty over the winter months and the restaurant is quiet after the frantic Christmas period. For us it's time for a short break as we get away, take the team skiing and reflect back upon the year.

We don't rest on our laurels for too long though and we grab the chance to do a spot of maintenance at this point in the year. Thorough cleaning of the restaurant and guestrooms ensues with a lick of paint here and there to keep things looking spick and span.

Sussex House down the road also needs its fair share of TLC so stables are repaired and any extra fencing is added to keep the animals safe and sound. It's typical Winteringham Fields team work, with the boys, Bex and even our daughters mucking in where possible, making it feel a whole lot less like work and more like quality time together.

In the garden, trees are trimmed and the seating areas prepared for sunnier times to come.

Forward thinking is key during the winter and I start planning the planting scheme for the year while I'm finalising my autumn menus. Then, towards the end of the season life kicks into gear for Valentine's Day at the restaurant (which is always bedlam!) giving us a taste of things to come over the months ahead.

Leek velouté

Serves 8-10.

Ingredients

500g leeks, sliced
250ml whole milk
100ml double cream
100g unsalted butter
2 tsp fine sea salt

Method

Wash the leeks, top and tail then slice around ½cm thick.

Melt the butter in a saucepan on a low heat and add the leeks.

Cover with a cartouche, this is a disc of greaseproof paper that acts as a lid. Soften the leeks on a low heat for 10-15 minutes.

After this time add the milk, cream and salt and bring to the boil slowly.

When boiled, remove from the heat and blitz in a blender.

Pass through a fine sieve and serve hot.

Foie gras three ways
with textures of quince

Ingredients

For the foie gras brûlée

150g foie gras

2 egg yolks

3 eggs

250ml double cream

25ml brandy

1 tsp honey

50g Demerara sugar

For the foie gras

1 lobe of foie gras

Large knob of butter

Sprig of thyme

½ garlic clove, crushed

For the pasta dough

1 whole egg

9 egg yolks

500g type 00 flour

25ml olive oil

40ml water

For the quince pieces and purée

3 quinces

150g sugar

300ml water

1 vanilla pod

For the Port reduction

250ml Port

50g caster sugar

For the blown wild rice

50g wild rice

Vegetable oil for deep frying

For the foie gras ravioli filling

40g foie gras, trimmings

100g treacle

Pinch of salt

Method

For the foie gras brûlée

Get all the ingredients to room temperature and blitz until fully smooth and combined.

Pass through a fine sieve and then pour into little ramekins.

Cook in a bain-marie in the oven at 100°c for 45 minutes.

Place in the fridge to cool down.

Blitz up the Demerara sugar so it is very fine.

Serve the brûlée at room temperature, sprinkle with the fine sugar and blowtorch, or place under a hot grill, until you have a perfect almost glass layer.

For the foie gras

Portion the foie gras into 50g pieces, save any trim for the ravioli.

Place a heavy-based ovenproof frying pan on a medium heat.

Season both sides of the foie gras and place in the pan. You do not need any oil as the foie gras is very fatty.

Once the side has a golden brown colour flip over and put the butter, thyme and garlic into the pan.

The butter will start to foam so baste the foie gras quickly and then place the pan in the oven at 180°c for 1 minute to cook through.

Carefully take the pan out of the oven and baste for another 20 seconds. Season with a pinch more salt and then serve.

For the foie gras ravioli filling

Rub the foie gras and treacle together with a pinch of salt.

Gently warm through in a bowl over a pan of hot water. Do this for about 10 minutes to start letting the fat out of the foie gras.

Leave to cool and then ball in to 15g pieces small enough to fill the ravioli.

For the pasta dough

Slowly combine the whole egg and yolks to the flour, either by hand using a whisk or with an electric mixer.

Next add the olive oil and and mix until fully combined. The flour should all be the same colour.

Bring together and knead until smooth. Wrap in cling film and place in the fridge to relax for 30 minutes.

Roll out the pasta to thin sheets, or if using a pasta machine then to number 1, slowly going down from 10. When at number 1 pass the pasta sheet through twice.

Cut out your ravioli with a 7½cm round cutter.

Take two discs and place a ball of foie gras into the middle of the bottom one. Brush the edges of the pasta discs with a little water so they stick then cover the bottom disc with another piece of pasta and then press to form a ravioli. Make as many as your pasta and filling will allow as you can always freeze them for another day.

For the quince pieces and purée

Halve and deseed the vanilla pod, place in to a saucepan with the sugar and water then bring to the boil. This will make a stock syrup.

Place the quince into the stock syrup on a very low heat and cook overnight at 80°c.

When cooled, take two of the quince and peel the skin off and remove the middle, which are grainy, then place in a blender and blitz. Add a little stock syrup if needed to get a smooth purée. Pass through a fine sieve to remove any bits.

Place into a piping bag or squeeze bottle for serving.

Peel the remaining quince then slice large flat pieces from around the sides and then dice to size you require.

To serve, place the quince the pieces under a grill or in the oven to warm through and then place on top of the cooked foie gras.

For the Port reduction

Place ingredients into a saucepan on a medium to low heat.

Stir until all the sugar is dissolved.

Reduce slowly until like a syrup. Place into a squeezy bottle for serving.

For the blown wild rice

In a deep saucepan fill a quarter of the way up with vegetable oil and heat to 190°c.

When the oil is up to temperature gently drop in the wild rice. It will puff up quickly and spit a little so be very careful when removing from the pan.

Season lightly and place on kitchen cloth to remove some of the oil.

To serve place over the top of the quince pieces on the foie gras.

Smoked mussel risotto with Parmesan tuille

Serves 8.

Ingredients

For the smoked mussel stock

500g mussels
350ml white wine
1 carrot, grated
300ml water
1 onion, diced
500ml fish stock
1 carrot, diced

For the risotto

300g Arborio rice
150g shallots, brunoised
2 garlic cloves, crushed
150ml white wine
30ml vegetable oil
1 bay leaf
2 sprigs of thyme
600ml smoked mussel stock
Salt, to taste
(Continued overleaf)

Method

For the smoked mussel stock

In a large pan heat some oil to a very high temperature then add the grated carrot and half of the onion and stir until it starts to colour. Then add the mussels and shake around.

After 10 seconds add 150ml white wine, then after another 10 seconds add the water.

Cook until the shells are fully open and discard any that do not open.

Pass through a colander and save the stock.

Pick out all the mussels from the shells and then smoke. You can do this either with a smoke gun by cling filming the hose into a container which is fully cling filmed, or by using a big bowl with hay in the bottom. For this, put the mussels in a colander, light the hay and then cover with the colander and cling film fully. Do this twice for 20 minutes at a time.

In a pan sweat off the other half of the onion and diced carrots until they are light brown in colour.

Add the mussels and continue to cook for 30 seconds on a medium to high heat.

Add in the rest of the white wine and reduce by half.

Then add the left over stock and fish stock and simmer for 15 minutes.

Quickly blitz in a blender and then pass through a fine sieve or chinois.

Reserve the stock for later use.

For the risotto

In a pan with oil sweat off the shallots on a medium to low heat so they do not colour.

Add the Arborio rice and mix well to coat in the oil.

Add the garlic cloves, thyme and bay leaf.

Add in the wine and reduce until almost gone on a medium heat, while continuously stirring with a spatula.

Pour in the stock and cook on a medium heat until almost fully cooked through. To test, squeeze one grain between your finger and thumb and if it splits into three parts it is ready.

Season with salt to taste.

Lay on a flat tray in the fridge. This will cool it quicker. (Continued overleaf.

Smoked mussel risotto
with Parmesan tuille (continued)

Ingredients

For the fresh mussels

100g mussels

15ml oil

150ml white wine

For the Parmesan tuille

200g Parmesan

For the saffron cromesque

Pinch of saffron

1 litre fish stock

1 tbsp dashi powder

100g cornflour

1 tbsp water

100g flour

250g panko breadcrumbs

3 eggs

Oil, for deep frying

Method

For the fresh mussels

In a heavy-based saucepan heat the oil to a high temperature.

Add in the mussels.

Add in the wine and cover with a lid, shake around and cook off for 30 seconds to 1 minute.

Pass into a colander.

Pick out of the shells making sure they are perfect by removing any beards, and also so they hold their natural shape.

Cool in the fridge until needed.

To heat up place the mussels in a small pan with some stock, then add a pinch of cream to create a creamy sauce.

Serve hot onto of the risotto with a little sauce in and around it.

For the Parmesan tuille

Remove all the rind from the Parmesan and discard.

Finely grate some Parmesan onto a non-stick baking mat on an oven tray.

Do enough so it is almost half a centimetre deep, push in around the edges so the edge of the mat is showing.

Cook in the oven at 180°c for 4 minutes.

Remove from the oven and leave to cool on the tray to set.

Turn out onto a chopping board and portion in half and then into thin rectangles.

Put back onto the non-stick baking mat and back in the oven for 3 to 4 minutes into a firm crisp tuille.

When cool decorate with 3 small pieces of dill and serve over the top of the risotto.

For the saffron cromesque

Add the fish stock and saffron into a saucepan and bring to the boil.

Take off the heat and blitz with a hand blender to break down the saffron.

Mix the corn flour with water in a bowl then pour into the saffron mix and whisk in.

Continually whisk on a medium heat until it thickens. When it thickens whisk and cook out for a further 5 minutes.

Set into a small rectangle tray and put into the freezer.

When frozen blow torch the metal base, or place into hot water, then turn out onto a chopping board and cut into 1 inch cubes.

Cover in flour and dust off any excess.

Beat 3 eggs and then dip the floured cube in to completely coat, then drain off any excess on a cloth.

Roll in panko breadcrumbs and then freeze until needed.

To serve, deep fry at 190°c for 2 minutes.

Balmoral venison with red cabbage and venison sausage

In the correct season wild venison is such a joy to have on the menu. We simply pair it with some red cabbage and celeriac, serving the meat in a way that accentuates its great flavour. We ensure we have no wastage by using all the trim of this wonderful meat.

Ingredients

For the celeriac purée

500g celeriac
100g butter
300ml whole milk
100ml double cream
1 tsp salt

For the potato pavé

10 potatoes
1 block clarified butter
Salt and pepper, to season
250g Gruyère cheese, grated

For the red cabbage

250g red cabbage
50g onion
100g carrots
50ml double cream
25g butter
Salt, to taste

For the venison sausage

250g venison trim
50g pork fat
25g panko breadcrumbs
1 tsp salt
Pinch of nutmeg, ground
Pinch of cinnamon, ground
70ml water
Caul fat (optional)

For the venison loin

100g venison loin
10g butter
Sprig of thyme
1 garlic clove, crushed
Pinch salt and pepper

Method

For the celeriac purée.
Dice up the celeriac into small pieces.
In a heavy-based saucepan melt the butter on a low to medium heat.
When the butter is all melted but is not coloured, add in the celeriac, make a cartouche and cover, then cook on a low heat for 10 minutes.
Once soft add in the milk and cream and bring up to the boil slowly.
Take off the heat and add in the salt, blitz then pass through a sieve.
Put into a squeeze bottle for serving.

For the potato pavé.
Wash and peel the potatoes, then thinly slice on a mandoline.
On parchment paper on an oven tray, start to do one layer of potato into a square shape. With a pastry brush, brush clarified butter over the layer of potatoes, season with salt and pepper and sprinkle over a fine layer of cheese evenly.
Keep repeating until you have a fairly deep square with plenty of layers.
Fold over the parchment paper to cover the top so it does not dry out and cook at 160°c for 40 minutes.
Place in the fridge between 2 trays or plates to compress all of the layers together.
Once set and solid, trim off the stray edges and then portion into thin rectangle shapes.
In a frying pan with a little oil on a medium heat start to colour the inside piece. This way, as it turns golden brown it will show off all the layers.
Serve from the pan hot.

For the red cabbage.
Finely chop the onions and sweat off in a little oil for 4 minutes, making sure they are soft but there is no colour.
Grate the carrots and add into the pan, then sweat for another 2 minutes.
Next grate the cabbage and add this to the pan. Mix through well and add the butter. Keep on a fairly low heat and cook off for 5-10 minutes.
Add salt and cream while still on the heat, then mix until all combined.
Serve hot.

To make the venison sausage.
If you do not have a mincer or sausage machine you can ask your butcher to do you a venison and pork sausage mix and then mix through everything apart from the water after.
Mince together the venison trim and pork fat, put through twice each time adding a little bit of cold water (cold water prevents the meat from going grey).
When you are happy with the coarseness, add to a mixing bowl with the panko breadcrumbs, nutmeg, cinnamon and salt.
Mix well. If you have a sausage machine at this point put it back through the machine with the filling attachment on and the pig intestine skin around to form the sausage.
If not, just roll into the preferred size and either wrap in caul fat and fry without any skin.
Colour in a pan and gently cook through from a low heat.
Serve when cooked. We use a piece of Douglas fir pushed in (this also gives a slight fragrance to the sausage).

For the venison loin.
Take the loin and trim off any fat and sinew. Season all over with salt and pepper evenly.
In a frying pan on medium to high heat, colour all the sides, in order to get a dark brown colour.
Place the loin, butter, thyme and garlic on a tray and then put into the oven at 100°c. Cook with a temperature probe in until the middle is 48°c.
Take out of the oven and roll in the butter, cover with tin foil and rest for around 10 minutes. This helps the meat to relax.
Slice into 2-3 slices, season and serve.

Lemon sole with caper salsa

Lobster and lemon sole work tremendously well together. The three major components of this dish are the delicate lemon sole itself, this goes great with the simple salsa and a lobster croquette.

Serves 4.

Ingredients

For the lemon sole

1 lemon sole

Pinch of salt

Knob of butter

1 tsp lemon juice

For the caper salsa

20g banana shallot

28g baby capers

40g cucumber

40g wakame seaweed

16g dashi powder

20ml vegetable oil

For the sour cream

600ml double cream

3 whole lemons, juiced

15g chopped dill

Salt, to taste

For the Pernod grapes

300ml water

100ml olive oil

90ml lemon juice

60g sugar

6 star anise

Sprig of thyme

2 tbsp Pernod

Punnet of green grapes, peeled

For the fennel slices

1 head fennel

Drizzle Pernod dressing

Pinch of salt

Method

For the lemon sole.

Either ask your fishmonger to fillet for you – or follow the instructions overleaf.

Season the side where the skin was, and then in a very hot frying pan with oil, place it seasoned side down.

It will cook very fast so as you see it start to cook through, add a knob of butter, flip over, then add a squeeze of lemon juice. Keep for 10 seconds like this then take out and serve.

For the caper salsa.

Soak the seaweed in hot water until rehydrated.

Peel the cucumber and then slice on a mandoline or with a knife. Slice all the way around the middle so not to get any of the middle bits.

Brunoise (very finely dice) the cucumber and shallots and put in a mixing bowl.

Drain off the water from the seaweed and add it into the shallot and cucumber mix.

Add the baby capers.

In a separate tray mix the oil and dashi powder, then add into the mixing bowl.

Serve at room temperature on the base of the plate.

For the sour cream.

Add the cream and lemon juice into a bowl.

Whisk the cream and whip it till it firms up (make sure not to over whip).

Finely chop the dill sprigs, add to the cream and mix in gently.

Add a pinch of salt to taste.

For the Pernod grapes.

Peel the grapes and then halve them then mix all of the ingredients together.

For the fennel slices.

Quarter the fennel and trim off the top pieces.

Slice very finely on a mandoline.

Put into ice water to make it as crunchy as possible.

Just before serving, place on a tray and dress with a little of the Pernod dressing and a pinch of salt and allow to warm to room temperature. (Continued...)

Lemon sole
with caper salsa (continued)

Ingredients

For the lobster bisque

3 lobster bones

25g carrots

25g onions

25g mushrooms

25g celery

25g leeks

2 cloves garlic

2 sprigs of thyme

1 bay leaf

Parsley

Pinch saffron

50ml brandy

100ml white wine

2 litres fish stock or water

250ml double cream

100g tomato purée

For the lobster croquette

500ml lobster bisque

50g cornflour

lobster pieces (1g times however many pieces need)

250g panko bread crumbs

3 eggs, beaten

100g flour

Pinch salt

Method

For the lobster bisque.

Wash and dry lobster bones.

Roast lobster in the oven at 100°c for 30 minutes.

In the pan, colour all of the vegetables until golden brown, then add tomato purée and cook for 3 minutes.

Add the lobster bones and cook for 2 minutes.

Add the brandy and blowtorch to burn the alcohol off.

Add white wine and reduce until almost dry.

Add the fish stock and herbs, then cook for 1 hour on medium heat.

Add double cream and cook for 20 minutes.

Infuse for 1 hour, pass through a chinois then blitz in a blender to mix it.

For the lobster croquette.

In a pan add the lobster bisque and cornflour and whisk in.

Place on a medium heat and continually whisk.

The mix will start to thicken. Keep cooking for around 5 minutes and keep whisking.

Place the mix into a piping bag and set up a plastic flexi small dome moulds.

Fill in the moulds but leave a little bit of room in each for a small lobster piece. Press it into the mix and then put in the freezer.

When frozen, pop all of them out of the mould and cover them in flour, shaking off any excess.

Next coat them in the egg mix and place on a J-cloth to strain slightly.

Roll around in the panko bread crumbs until they are completely covered.

Deep fry at around 180-190°c for 1-2 minutes.

Season with a pinch of salt and serve.

To fillet the lemon sole

Place the lemon sole face side up and make a cut down the middle along the spine.

Either side of the spine is a fillet so using a filleting knife, run it all the way from the top to the bottom against the bone. This will take off of the maximum meat the fillet.

Once both fillets are off, turnover and repeat the process.

Now remove the skin from the fillet; start from the tail end of the fillet cutting in and down to the skin.

Run the knife flat across the skin all the way through in a smooth sawing motion.

Bex's lazy days
chicken stew and dumplings

This stew in made by my wife Bex and is a real family favourite of ours. One of the great things about this dish is that you can use any meat, and any vegetables that you have in your fridge and still get a great and hearty meal.

Serves 8.

Ingredients

1 chicken carcass, with some meat still on

A selection of your favourite seasonal vegetables

Baked potato or frozen dumplings

Extra chicken breasts

2 white onions

250ml white wine

2 tbsp Bisto gravy granuales

Method

Take your old chicken carcass after a Sunday roast (the more meat left on, the better!) chuck it in a pan of water and let it simmer away for 2 hours on a medium heat, while you watch a movie.

If you are doing Sunday lunch get the children to chop up extra vegetables. My lot are great at this because they chop everything into tiny pieces which are great for a stew (not so good for a roast!). We use anything from cabbage to carrots.

Sieve the chicken keeping the water. I hate stew with bones in it; chefs seem to love them in a stew but I think it's awful to come across them when you just want a good mouthful. Pull the meat from the bones and drop back into the water.

A few extra chicken breast fillets will get a bit more meat into the mix. Fry them off with some onions, add the wine, and fry until the alcohol has burnt off. Then add the chicken broth water and of all your vegetables. I use the blasphemous Bisto to thicken it up a bit then leave it to it.

I generally get set upon by Colin and a load of chefs at this point, but the way to make it go further is either with baked potatoes or by popping in a bag of Aunt Bessie's frozen dumplings.

If my children are looking interested I will make my own but by this point I have lost them to being thrown around the room by the boys, so good old Aunt Bessie's is my secret. Put it the oven for 30 minutes on a high heat.

It's a meal in a bowl and it keeps Colin going for most of the week in leftovers.

Partridge with truffle polenta, parsnip and pancetta

Serves 4.

Ingredients

For the parsnip purée

500g parsnips
300ml double cream
300ml whole milk
100g butter
Salt, to taste

For the truffle polenta

2 shallots, finely diced
1 garlic clove, finely diced
Vegetable oil
100g unsalted butter
150g coarse polenta
1 litre chicken stock
1 tsp salt
100ml double cream
1 tsp truffle oil
Parmesan cheese

For the creamed sprouts

500g sprouts
50g butter
2 white onions, finely diced
100ml double cream
4 rashers smoked bacon, finely chopped
Salt to taste

For the sprout leaves

20 sprout leaves, 5 per portion
Emulsion from the sprouts

For the partridge

1 partridge, whole
15g butter
Pinch of salt and pepper
Sprig of thyme
1 garlic clove, crushed

For the pancetta

25g pancetta, cubed
15g butter
10ml water

Method

For the parsnip purée.

Wash, peel and dice the parsnips.

In a deep saucepan, slowly melt the butter then add the diced parsnip and cover with a cartouche (simply a disc of greaseproof paper). Cook on a very low heat for 10 minutes.

Remove the cartouche and add in the milk and cream, then slowly simmer for a further 5 minutes.

Place in a blender, blitz then pass through a sieve.

Season with salt to taste.

For the truffle polenta.

Finely dice the shallots and garlic.

In a saucepan sweat the shallots and garlic in a little vegetable oil. When soft add the butter and melt.

Add in the polenta, chicken stock and salt.

Cook out on a low simmer for 20 minutes while continually whisking.

Add the cream and truffle oil then whisk and cook for a further minute. Check seasoning again.

Rub a little oil on to a small rectangular tray, then set the polenta in it and place in the fridge.

When set portion into 1 inch squares. Finely grate the Parmesan over the top of each square and grill until golden brown.

For the creamed sprouts.

Wash and remove the first layer of sprout leaves and retain.

Trim and slice the sprouts in half from the stalks.

In a saucepan make a butter emulsion with three quarters of a pan of water, a block of butter and salt. Cook the sprouts until soft, around 5 minutes and save the emulsion for later.

Allow to cool slightly and then finely chop the cooked sprouts.

Slowly sweat off the onions in a pan with a little oil.

Finely chop the smoked bacon and add this to the onions along with the cooked sprouts.

Finally add in the cream and reduce. Season and serve.

For the sprout leaves.

Use the emulsion retained from cooking the sprouts.

Place the saucepan on the stove on a low heat and simmer the emulsion.

Drop the sprout leaves into the emulsion for 20 seconds and serve immediately.

For the partridge.

Pluck the feathers from the partridge breast. With a sharp knife, carefully remove the breast from the crown. Wash any remaining feathers from the breast. Season the top of the breast with salt and pepper.

Place a frying pan on a medium heat, add a splash of oil and place the breast into the hot pan. After 3 minutes add a knob of butter, a sprig of thyme and the crushed garlic.

Baste the breast with the butter and cook for a further minute.

Leave to rest for 5 minutes then slice the breast down the middle from top to bottom and glaze with the pan juices.

For the pancetta.

Cut a 2cm cube from the pancetta. Remove the skin, seal in a frying pan.

Turnover and add the butter. When the butter starts to foam, add the water to create an emulsion and baste the pancetta until cooked.

Serve immediately while hot.

Cod and oxtail
with lemon butter sauce

Serves 4.

Ingredients

1 side of cod

Herb salt

25g butter

Vegetable oil, enough for the pan

For the oxtail rillettes

2kg oxtail

100g tomato purée

500ml red wine

1 onion

1 carrot

1 leek

2 garlic cloves, crushed

Sprig of thyme

1 bay leaf

Water to cover

For the oxtail sauce

Oxtail stock, retained from rillettes

For the confit potatoes

4 potatoes

Butter or oil

1 garlic clove, crushed

Sprig of thyme

Salt

For the shallots

4 banana shallots

Salt

Oil

Sprig of thyme

Large knob of butter

For the lemon butter sauce

2 shallots, finely chopped

1 tsp garlic, mined

250ml white wine

250ml fish stock

250ml double cream

15ml lemon juice

½ lemon, zest only

Caviar, to finish

Butter, to finish

Salt, to taste

Method

Trim any fatty bits off the cod, cut down the middle and then skin.

Salt the cod with a coarse herb salt, evenly spread all over then leave the for 25 minutes. Wash off the salt and leave to dry on a clean tea towel in the fridge. Portion the cod into 100g pieces.

Cook in a heavy-based frying pan on a medium to high heat, add a little vegetable oil and place the cod skin side down (there is no skin on but the side the skin would have been on).

When golden brown add the butter and then cook for 30 seconds more.

Turn over and place on a tray in the oven at 180°c for 1-2 minutes.

For the oxtail rillettes.

Roast the oxtail at 200°c for 20 minutes. Turn over every 5 minutes to colour evenly.

Next, finely dice the carrot, onion, leek and garlic to create a mirepoix. Cook this off in a large pan with a little oil on a medium heat. When golden brown add the tomato purée, reduce the heat and cook out slowly while stirring.

Add the oxtail into the pan and turn the heat to medium, stir to fully combine. Add the red wine and reduce by half, then add the herbs and cover completely with water.

Bring up to the boil and then turn down to a low simmer with a lid for 4 hours.

Remove from the heat and leave to rest for 20 minutes.

When cooked pass through a colander and reserve the stock to reduce later.

Pick the oxtail by removing any gristle or cartilage into a separate bowl then season with salt and pepper.

Lay three pieces of cling film flat overlapping each other, place the oxtail mixture to the closest edge to you of the cling film then roll as tight as possible and tie off each end, removing the air as you go.

Set in the fridge for at least 2 hours.

To serve, cut a portion then fry top and bottom on a medium heat and then into the oven to warm through.

For the oxtail sauce.

Reduce the retained oxtail stock until thick.

For the confit potatoes.

Wash and peel the potatoes.

Preheat enough fat to cover the potatoes to around 80°c in a saucepan. Add the garlic and thyme.

Use a melon baller to scoop perfect ball shapes and then drop them into the oil or butter and cook for 20 minutes or until soft.

Season with salt and serve hot.

For the shallots.

Peel and halve the shallots, trim the root down but do not fully remove as it will not hold together.

In a frying pan on a medium heat add the oil and sprinkle some salt in, place the shallot in the pan and cook until an even dark golden brown colour.

Add in the butter and thyme and a pinch of water to emulsify and cook for a further minute. Flip over for another minute and cook until soft.

For the lemon butter sauce.

On a medium heat add the oil to a pan and sweat the diced shallots and garlic. When soft add the white wine and reduce by half then add the stock and reduce by half again.

Add the cream and reduce on a lower heat by a third.

Add the lemon juice and zest.

Remove from the heat and season. Slightly under season as when you finish the sauce you will add the caviar.

To serve gently heat and whisk in small cold knobs of butter until thickened add caviar and serve hot.

Frangipane with vanilla ice cream

Serves 4.

Ingredients

For the pâté a Breton

150g caster sugar

250g plain flour

200g unsalted butter

80g egg yolks, at room temperature

8g baking powder

1 vanilla pod, seeds only

For the mulled wine

1 bottle red wine

½ orange

60g caster sugar

1 cinnamon stick

1 star anise

1 tsp nutmeg, grated

For the pears in mulled wine

2 Williams pears

Mulled wine

For the vanilla ice cream

800ml whole milk

200ml double cream

200g egg yolks

200g sugar

5 vanilla pods

For the frangipane

500ml cream

225g unsalted butter

225g caster sugar

350g eggs

225g almond powder

75g plain flour, sifted

2 vanilla pods

50ml rum

Method

For the pâté a Breton.

Sift the flour and baking powder into a bowl.

Cream together the sugar and butter until light and fluffy. If you have an electric whisk this will make it easier.

Add in one egg yolk at a time, making sure they are full combined.

Add the vanilla seeds and continue to whisk.

Stop the mixer, add in the flour and baking powder then slowly mix in to prevent the flour from flying everywhere.

Bring the pastry together and wrap in cling film. Leave to rest in a fridge for 20 minutes.

Roll out the pastry thinly and cut out to the size of your tart case.

Press into the cases all the way around the edges so it is perfectly covered with no rips or air pockets. Place cling film on the inside of the tart and fill with dried beans or rice then blind bake in the oven for 6-8 minutes at 180°c.

For the mulled wine.

Add the wine, sugar, orange and spices into a saucepan and slowly bring to a simmer until all the sugar has dissolved

Remove from the heat and leave to infuse for 1-2 hours.

Set aside in an airtight container for later.

For the pears in mulled wine.

Pour the mulled wine into a saucepan and bring up to a gentle simmer.

Peel the pears and cut into 8 pieces, making sure to remove any pips.

Place the cut pears into the hot mulled wine and simmer for approximately 10 minutes, if the pears are really ripe it will take less time.

Place the pears into a container in the fridge to cool.

For the vanilla ice cream.

Split the vanilla pods and de-seed. In a saucepan put the milk and double cream and then all the vanilla pods and the seeds.

Infuse the milk and cream for 30 minutes then bring to a gentle boil.

In a separate bowl whisk the egg yolks and sugar until combined and pale.

When the milk and cream has boiled, remove from the stove to cool for a few minutes and then pour one third into the yolks and sugar. Whisk vigorously so it does not scramble.

Pour the rest of the milk and cream in and whisk until combined.

Place the pan back onto the heat and cook out to 83°c.

Pass through a fine sieve then pour into an ice cream maker.

If you do not have an ice cream maker, then pour into a tub and place in the freezer. Whisk every hour to keep it soft until fully frozen.

For the frangipane.

Halve and scrape out the seeds from vanilla pods.

In a mixing bowl, whisk the vanilla seeds, butter, sugar and cream until light and fluffy.

Add the eggs slowly one by one, each time making sure the eggs are fully combined in to the mix. This might be easier in you use an electric mixer.

Slowly add in the almonds, sifted flour and rum.

Mix until fully incorporated then fill your tart cases with the frangipane mix. Make sure it is nice and even. Place two pieces of the mulled pears into the frangipane mix.

Cook in the oven at 180°c for 12-15 minutes.

Serve straight from the oven with some clotted cream or ice cream.

Passion fruit soufflé

This dish has been on the Winteringham Fields menu for a long time. It is a dish that we trust and is a dish we can rely on to deliver flavour and excitement with a bit of theatrics.
The delicate soufflé with a cone of vanilla ice cream being pierced through the centre that slowly melts as you eat is truly a delight. Serves 4.

Ingredients

Passion fruit mix

500g passion fruit purée

70g sugar

50g cornflour

For the meringue base

240g egg whites

190g sugar

100g passion fruit mix

For the vanilla ice cream cone

800ml whole milk

200ml double cream

200g egg yolks

200g sugar

5 vanilla pods

Method

For the passion fruit mix.

Add all the ingredients into a pan.

Cook out on a medium heat continually whisking until the cornflour i cooked out and the mix is thick, glossy and smooth.

Cool in fridge with cling film pressed onto it to cover. This will prevent skin forming.

For the meringue base.

Make a firm meringue with egg whites and sugar.

Whisk half the meringue with passion fruit mix, and then slowly fold in th other half with a spatula.

Pour into soufflé moulds and level with a palate knife.

Pinch the mould edge with thumb and finger, running your nail thinl around the edge to create a divot.

Cook at 180°c for 8 minutes.

For the vanilla ice cream cone.

Halve and de-seed the vanilla pods and put with the milk and cream into pan. Leave to infuse for 10 minutes.

Bring the milk and cream to the boil.

Whisk the egg yolks and sugar in a bowl, until pale and all combined wit the sugar.

Pour a third of the milk and cream over the egg yolks and sugar and whisl really well. Add it all back into the pan and cook slowly up to 84°c.

Pass through a chinois or fine sieve to remove vanilla pods and into an ic cream churner or a container into the freezer, whisking every hour until set

When frozen but still a little soft, push into cones made from acetate sheet and freeze to create the cone shape.

Cherry clafoutis

Serves 4.

Ingredients

2 large eggs

100g sugar

6 tbsp crème fraîche

6 tbsp whole milk

48 cherries, whole or with pips removed

Soft butter, for greasing

Icing sugar, for dusting

Method

Preheat your oven to 220°c. Lightly grease four ramekins and place in the cherries. In a bowl whisk the eggs until frothy, this usually takes 1-2 minutes. Place the cherries into the oven for 5 minutes until soft. Meanwhile, finish the batter by adding the crème fraîche, milk and sugar then set aside. Once the cherries are soft and hot, pour in the batter and reduce the temperature to 186°c. Cook for 20 minutes until well risen.

Remove from the oven and dust with icing sugar.

The Quail
In The Woods

"Birds of a feather flock together"

Early one October morning I was out in the woods at the bottom of the fields and the mist was swirling through the trees, sinking slowly to the damp woodland floor so I could barely even see my feet. Suddenly the eerie silence was broken by the distinctive, shrill call of the quail Alan was rearing in his pens ready for the local shoot.

The sound of the birds and the smell of the damp woods gave me an idea. How could this snapshot of country life be translated into a starter course on my menu? 'The Quail in the Woods', which has gone on to become one of my signature dishes, started at this moment.

I needed to replicate the feelings evoked by my senses that morning into a recipe that would recreate the scene and the mood. It had to be visual, but not in a straight-forward way. I had to find a way of painting a picture on a plate that would represent the woodland floor, the mist and the quail. To lift the senses and recreate the eeriness of it all was my ultimate aim.

The dish is very visual and suggestive. The autumn woodland floor is represented by moss, wild flowers, and dehydrated black olives that replicate the soil. The scented aroma of bark stock provides the smell of the woodland floor and finally, liquid nitrogen provides the swirling mist. (Disclaimer: Bryony and Bex think this bit is Colin's Wordsworth moment and left it in for you all to have a giggle!)

It is a dish that recreates a little part of my life at Winteringham and I am very proud of it.

But the result is the perfect introduction to our philosophy and it never fails to impress when it comes out of the kitchen and into our restaurant.

I used 'The Quail in the Woods' in my debut in the Great British Menu TV programme in 2012. It was my first appearance on the show and I was really nervous. They wanted something groundbreaking and aesthetically stunning so this is what I did. It seemed to do the trick, as I won the regional heat and managed to get through to represent our region with the starter course on the menu at the Great British Olympic Banquet, held at the Old Royal Naval College in Greenwich.

I returned to the Great British Menu the following year, winning the regional heat, and in 2014 reached the final again where I created 'Homage to the Dickin Medal', for the D-Day banquet at St Paul's Cathedral. The real medal is the highest award for animals in warfare, their version of the Victoria Cross.

Quail in the woods

Roasted quail breast, tempura of its own egg, confit of its leg and parfait of its liver and foie gras garnished with foraged ingredients with black garlic cream and horseradish pearls.

This was my first winning banquet dish on Great British Menu and one of the dishes I get asked about most often. Serves 8. This dish takes over 36 hours to make in total.

Ingredients

For the quail breast

4 whole quail, head, entrails and legs removed
120g butter
4 sprigs of thyme
4 garlic cloves

For the quail egg kebab

8 quail eggs
50g flour
Cooked quail trim from breast

For the tempura batter

125g rice flour
10g baking powder
250ml sparkling water
25ml vodka

For the black garlic cream

60g black garlic
120g shallots
1 tsp thyme, leaves only
1 tsp rosemary, leaves only
100ml cream

For the quail sauce

10 quails, heads and entrails removed
25ml grapeseed oil
25g unsalted butter
1 shallot, finely sliced
2 star anise, crushed
300ml chicken bouillon
1 tsp black peppercorns, crushed
100ml Madeira
1 tsp Armagnac

Method

For the quail breast.
In a hot pan, sear the quail on each breast and then on the crown until golden brown.
Add the butter to the pan, stand quail up on its back and stuff with the thyme and garlic. Baste in the pan with the butter for 1 minute.
Place in a 120°c oven for 4 minutes and then rest for 15 minutes.
Remove breasts when rested and then set aside until needed.

For the tempura batter.
Combine all the ingredients together then mix.

For the quail egg kebab.
Bring a pan of water to the boil, place eggs in water and cook for 1 minute 50 seconds. Remove and keep in ice bath, then peel and dry the eggs.
Roll in the flour and dip in tempura batter. When ready to serve deep fry for 30 seconds then skewer the tempura egg with the quail trim.

For the black garlic cream.
Halve the garlic bulbs and put all of the ingredients except for the cream in a tray. Cover with foil and bake for 1 hour.
Blitz in a blender, pass through a fine sieve then add cream.

For the quail sauce.
Using a powerful mincer or food processor, grind the quails, then set them aside.
Heat a small amount of grapeseed oil in a large pressure cooker or saucepan until very hot, then fry the quail meat until browned. If the pan gets too hot, deglaze with a small amount of water. Remove the quail meat from the pan, drain and set aside.

Add the butter, shallot and crushed star anise to the pan and cook on a medium heat, deglazing from time to time, until the shallots are caramelised. Return the quail meat and cover with the chicken bouillon topping up with water if necessary. Add the crushed peppercorns. Seal the pressure cooker, bring to full pressure and cook for 2 hours. If using a normal saucepan, seal and cook for twice as long at a simmer. Remove from the heat and leave to cool before opening.
Skim the fat from the top and pass the stock through a fine sieve lined with a double layer of damp muslin then cover and chill in the fridge. When chilled, remove any fat that has solidified on the surface, then transfer the stock to a tray and freeze until completely solid.
Once frozen, dip the tray briefly in warm water and turn out the stock on a perforated tray lined with two layers of muslin. Set this over a large container to catch the stock as it defrosts, and place in the fridge to thaw very slowly over 24-36 hours.
In the meantime, bring 75ml of the Madeira to a simmer and set it alight. Let the flame burn out and then reduce the alcohol by half.
Add the reduced Madeira to the reduced stock and chill quickly in an ice bath or blast chiller. When cold, place in a sealed container in the fridge for 12 hours.
Strain the stock then add the remaining 25ml Madeira and the Armagnac. Chill until needed.

Quail in the woods
(Continued)

Ingredients

For the horseradish pearls (optional)

300g horseradish cream

300ml cream

For the confit leg

12 legs

1 tbsp coarse salt

Sprig of rosemary

Sprig of thyme

½ clove garlic

30g salted butter

For the foie gras parfait

2 shallots, finely sliced

1 garlic clove, minced

3 sprigs of thyme, tied with string

150ml dry Madeira

150ml ruby Port

75ml white Port

50ml brandy

300g foie gras, trimmed weight

100g chicken livers, trimmed weight

3 tsp table salt

240g eggs

300g unsalted butter, melted

For the feuilles de brick log

1 block feuille de brick pastry

For the miso glaze

100ml white miso

250ml sake

250ml mirin

115g sugar

To garnish

Sorrel or penny wort

For the woods

½ a log of bark

A handful of cleaned moss

Foraged wild berries, flowers and herbs

Any other woodland effects that take your fancy

Method

For the horseradish pearls.
Blend the ingredients together and rest. Then put into a pipette and squeeze into liquid nitrogen and reserve until end of dish.

For the confit leg.
Place the legs on a tray then mix the salt, herbs and garlic together and pour over legs. Leave for 10 minutes then wash well under water. Pat dry and wrap tightly in cling film with the butter and cook in a water bath for 1 hour 30 minutes at 75°c, or simmer in a saucepan for the same amount of time. Alternatively if you have the equipment you can vacuum pack.
Remove and cool then trim and remove the thigh bones.

For the foie gras parfait.
Place the shallots, garlic and thyme in a pan with the Madeira, ruby Port, white Port and brandy. Set aside to marinate for 24 hours.
Heat the marinated mixture until nearly all the liquid has evaporated, stirring regularly to prevent the shallots and garlic from burning. Remove from the heat and discard the thyme.
Preheat a water bath to 50°c, or use a steamer. Cut the foie gras into pieces roughly the same size as the chicken livers. Put the livers, foie gras and table salt in a vacuum pac bag, or wrap in clingfilm. Put the eggs and the alcohol reduction in a second vacuum pac bag with the butter in a third. Seal all the bags under full pressure, then place in the water bath, or steam for 20 minutes. Remove the bags from the water bath. Take a tablespoon of fat rendered from the meat and reserve for serving. Combine the eggs, alcohol reduction and meats in a bowl and mix with a hand-held blender. Slowly blitz in the butter, then transfer to a blender and blend for 1-2 minutes at until emulsified, being careful not to incorporate too much air.
Preheat the oven to 100°c. Fill a bain-marie with 5cm water and place in the oven. Pass the meat mixture first through a coarse sieve and then through a fine one. Pour into a terrine dish and place in the bain-marie. After 15 minutes, start checking the temperature of the parfait. When it reaches 62-64°c in the centre, remove from the oven and allow to cool. Refrigerate for 24 hours before serving.

For the filo tubes.
Roll out the filo pastry thinly and then roll around a thin rolling pin or heat proof tube. Bake for 7 minutes until golden brown and cut to size, around 2 inches long whilst still warm.
When the tubes have cooled, pipe the chilled foie gras parfait into each tube.

For the miso glaze.
Add all of the ingredients together and reduce in pan until they are the consistency of syrup.

To serve.
Assemble the woods as per the picture.
Spoon the quail sauce and garlic purée on a plate and place the foie gras parfait filled tuille.
Set up the "woods" and lay over a leg board and finish the breast in a pan. Garnish with sorrel or penny wort then last minute sprinkle the horseradish pearls on plate.

Spring

The birds are singing and the days are finally getting longer and brighter as spring steps into gear. Winteringham is full of vitality at this time, abuzz with the noise of farmers' machinery indicating the arrival of the planting season.

Bex tends to her spring bedding to add a splash of colour to the entrance of the restaurant and in the yards around our accommodation. We now have 15 guest rooms, so there is plenty to do to make things look as welcoming as possible.

And of course it's the season of beginnings; new life appears on the farm and piglets and lambs are born, which as you can imagine is enormous fun to be around.

I spend my time fine tuning the menus and experimenting; as the produce begins to sprout, so too do my ideas. There's something about this season that motivates creativity and action, and some of the best ideas are cooked up round about now.

We also have a big event coming up – Mothers' Day – one of the busiest of the year and the time when restaurant bookings rocket back up to healthy levels.

Crab, kohlrabi, pickle, dill oil and pickled dill

Serves 8.

Ingredients

For the mayonnaise

2 egg yolks

1 tsp Dijon mustard

25ml white wine vinegar

200ml vegetable oil

For the picked crab

500g fresh crab

Mixing the crab

200g picked crab

75ml mayonnaise

Salt & pepper to season

1 lime

12 kohlrabies

For the pickle

250ml water

250ml white wine vinegar

250g sugar

1 star anise

6 peppercorns

3 bay leaves

4 cloves

For the dashi marinade

100ml vegetable oil

50ml kombu seaweed

½ lime, juiced

½ lime, zested

1 tsp sugar

For the garnish

25g dill

Method

For the mayonnaise.

Mix the egg yolks, vinegar and mustard together with a whisk, or electric mixer.

Slowly start adding in the oil while continually whisking until you have a very thick consistency.

Taste, then season with salt and pepper.

Pick the crabmeat.

Spread out the crabmeat in a large tray.

Pick the crab by pressing with your fingertips to make sure there is no shell or cartilage.

Repeat this process three times.

Mixing the crab.

Fold the crab and mayonnaise together. Add half the juice of one lime, and the zest of a whole lime.

Taste, then season with salt and pepper.

For the dashi marinade.

Combine all of the ingredients together in a bowl until the sugar has dissolved.

For the pickle.

Combine all of the ingredients in a pan and bring to the boil. Once the sugar has dissolved remove from the heat and allow to cool down. It is ready to use once it is completely cold.

Top and tail 8 kohlrabies then peel. Thinly slice into ribbons using a Japanese mandoline if you have one. Marinate in the dashi marinade and vacuum pack, or wrap in cling film.

Top and tail 4 kohlrabies and slice to 1.5mm thick, using a meat slicer if you have one. Stack 5 Kohlrabi discs on top of each other and using a £2 coin size cutter cut through. Marinate this in the pickle.

Using a pair of tweezers carefully pick nice sprigs of dill to use as a garnish.

Chilled pea and mint velouté & beetroot meringue with foie gras and apple purée

Serves 4.

Ingredients

For the velouté

1kg frozen garden peas

12g mint leaves

Salt

For the beetroot meringue

125ml water

50g beetroot powder, plus extra for sprinkling

125g pasteurised egg whites

100g sugar

50g maltodextrin (available online)

1.5g xanthan gum (available online)

2g egg white powder (available online)

Maldon sea salt, to season

For the foie gras parfait

400g foie gras

400g chicken livers

7 eggs

800g butter

250ml Madeira wine

250ml Port

75ml brandy

20g sea salt

1 bay leaf

Sprig of thyme

Sprig of rosemary

150g shallots, finely diced

For the apple purée

6 Granny Smith apples

Demerara sugar, for dusting

Apple juice if required

Method

For the velouté.

Defrost the peas at room temperature overnight in a colander over a bowl. The next day, mix with the mint and juice all together through a juicer. Pass the velouté through a fine sieve and season with salt to taste. Store in the fridge until chilled and serve as an appetiser or as a summer soup.

For the beetroot meringue.

Using the kitchen aid whisk the water and beetroot powder until well combined, then pour in the pasteurised egg whites and whisk until soft peaks form. Whilst this is whisking, separately add all of the other ingredients in together until well combined. Then put a spoon at a time of this into the meringue mixture until all of the powder is added.

Fill a piping bag fitted with a medium plain nozzle. Pipe the mixture into domes about 3cm tall on to a cling filmed dehydrator tray or oven sheet. Sprinkle with some more beetroot powder and Maldon sea salt and place into a dehydrator or oven at 58°c for 7–8 hours until completely dry. Once cooled, scoop out the bottom of the meringue with a melon baller and place into an air tight container until needed.

For the foie gras parfait.

Place the Madeira, Port, brandy, salt, bay leaf, thyme, rosemary and shallots into a heavy-based pan and reduce by half. Remove from the heat and leave to cool. Vacuum pack the foie gras and chicken livers separately (or wrap in cling film) and place into a water bath at 50°c for 20 minutes. Alternatively you can steam.

Remove from the water bath and place the eggs and the reduction into a blender and blitz for 1 minute. Add the foie gras and the livers and blitz for another minute then put it down to a low speed so the mixture is still turning. Slowly add the butter until it is all incorporated, then pass into a bowl and taste. Season if required, place into a terrine mould and cook in a bain-marie with a temperature probe in the centre of the parfait at 100°c. When 57°c is reached remove from the heat and chill. Once chilled, place into a piping bag and pipe into the bottom of the meringue.

For the apple purée.

Peel, core and roughly chop the apple. Place into a bowl and dust with Demerara sugar until well covered. Place a heavy bottom pan onto the stove and wait for it to get very hot, then add the sugar coated apples. Do not stir or move the apples for 2 minutes until the sugar has started to caramelise. Reduce the heat and continue to cook until the apples are soft and golden brown. If the mixture is a little dry add a bit of the apple juice. Now place the apple into the blender and blitz for 3 minutes to a smooth purée. Pass in to a bowl and chill. Place into a piping bag and serve with the parfait filled beetroot meringue and pea and mint velouté.

Foie gras, smoked eel and pork belly terrine with Pedro Ximénez jelly

Serves 12. This dish takes longer than 24 hours to make.

Ingredients

For the confit pork belly

1 whole pork belly, bone removed

250g butter

Herb salt to season

Pinch black peppercorns

Pinch coriander seeds

2 star anise

1 cinnamon stick

4 cloves

For the foie gras

4 lobes of fresh foie gras

100ml white Port

100ml Madeira wine

100ml brandy

1 pinch cayenne pepper

50ml honey

2 drops truffle oil

Sprig of thyme

Pink salt, to season

1 large smoked eel

For the Pedro jelly

800ml Pedro Ximénez sherry

4g agar agar

5 gelatine leaves

For the caramelised apple purée

6 apples, skin on but cored and chopped

250g Demerara sugar

To serve

2 Granny Smith apples – peeled, cored and cubed into 1cm cubes

Brioche (see page 206)

Method

For the confit pork belly.

Cut the belly pork in half width-ways and season with all of the spices and the herb salt. Place each half into its own vacuum bag, or wrap with cling film, with half of the butter in each one as well. Seal the bag and steam at 85°c overnight.

Once the pork is cooked, remove from the steamer and press in the fridge between two baking sheets with weight on the top until completely cold. Once cold, portion into 1 inch cube pieces and return to the fridge until needed.

For the foie gras.

Leave the fresh foie gras out at room temperature for 20 minutes and let it break down its natural line. Remove the thick vein from the middle of the liver then put it back together and slice into 1cm thick pieces. Place into a vacuum pack bag, (unsealed) or wrap in cling film and leave to one side.

In a pan combine the Port, Madeira, brandy, and flambé. Once the flame has died down, add the cayenne, honey, truffle oil, thyme and salt, then leave the marinade to cool. Once cool, pour the liquor over the foie gras and vacuum pack. Leave to marinate overnight.

The next day cook the foie gras in a water bath or steam at 50°c for 20 minutes. Whilst the foie gras is cooking prepare the eel by removing the head, back, skin and any remaining rib bones until you are left with just the fillets. Thinly slice the belly pork in long strips to 1.5mm and put with the eel. Line a square terrine mould with a double layer of cling film and secure tightly with sellotape.

Now the foie gras is cooked, pour half of it into the mould and lever out with a palate knife. Place in the freezer to set the top. Once set, start layering it up with the belly pork then add the eel and the remaining foie gras. Cover with cling film and set in the fridge overnight.

The next day, remove the cling film on the top and move the mould up a little so it's around 1cm above the terrine. Place in the freezer until the top is ice cold.

For the jelly.

Place the sherry and agar agar in a pan on a high heat and bring to the boil for 1 minute before removing from the heat. Soak the gelatine until soft, then squeeze out the excess water and add to the warm sherry. Whisk until dissolved. Allow to cool a little and pour on top of the ice cold terrine. Place in the fridge to set the jelly completely.

Once the jelly has set (approximately 30 minutes), remove from the fridge and with a hot knife carefully cut around the outside of the terrine, which should slide out. Place onto a chopping board and slice in half. Once you have got the two halves, cut into 1cm portions.

For the caramelised apple purée.

In a hot pan add the sugar and caramelise. Add the chopped apples and cook until a light caramel colour. Reduce the heat and allow to sweat until the mixture is mushy. Blend while warm until smooth.

Serve with fresh apple, caramelised apple purée and toasted brioche.

To make the brioche follow the recipe on page 206.

Lobster risotto

Ingredients

For the lobster bisque

6 lobster shells
50g carrots
50g onions
50g mushrooms
50g celery
50g leeks
4 garlic cloves
2 bay leaves
Small bunch parsley
100ml brandy
200ml white wine
4 litres fish stock/water
1 litre double cream
Pinch saffron
100ml tomato purée
2 litres water
50g tomato purée
500ml cream

For the risotto

300g Arborio rice
150ml white wine
100g chopped shallots
1 tbsp tomato purée
2 garlic cloves
2 bay leaves
Bunch of thyme
600ml fish/lobster stock
30ml vegetable oil

For the mango gel

1 litre mango purée
12g agar agar

For the lobster rock

Lobster stock
Cardamom pods
Star anise
Black peppercorns
Lobster trim
Tapioca starch
Sea salt

Method

For the lobster bisque.

Preheat the oven to 100°c. Wash and dry the lobster shells then roast in the oven for 30 minutes.

In a pan colour all of the vegetables until golden brown, then add the tomato purée and cook for 3 minutes. Add the lobster shells and cook for 2 minutes.

Add the brandy and blowtorch to burn the alcohol off. Add white wine and reduce until almost dry.

Add the fish stock, garlic, parsley, saffron and bay leaves then cook for 1 hour on medium heat.

Add the double cream and cook for 20 minutes.

Infuse for 1 hour, pass through a chinois then place in a blender.

To the shells add 2 litres of water, 50ml of tomato purée and 500ml cream. Cook for 30 minutes then pass through a chinois or fine sieve.

For the risotto.

Add together the shallots, garlic, vegetable oil, bay leaves and thyme. Add the tomato purée and cook for 2 minutes. Then add the rice and white wine. Add 450ml of stock and cook for 6 minutes, while stirring continuously. Add more stock if necessary. Cool it down on a tray in the fridge.

For the fresh mango.

Peel and dice the mango.

For the mango gel.

Mix the purée with the agar agar on boil, then set in the tray. Blitz in a blender until smooth. Keep in a vacuum pack bag, or wrap in cling film.

For the lobster rock.

Bring all of the ingredients except for the trim, tapioca and salt to the boil. Allow to cool to 70°c. Pass through a sieve or chinois and keep at 70°c.

Blitz the trim in a blender and pass through the drum sieve. Mix the fish, tapioca and salt together.

Combine all of the ingredients and knead until smooth and combined.

Roll out in cling film to 2cm thickness and steam for 1 hour on each side.

Cool down and slice. Dry for 1 hour then deep fry for 5 seconds.

Roast loin of lamb with confit belly pomme purée and aubergine

Ingredients

1 loin of lamb

Vegetable oil, for frying

Maldon sea salt

Knob of butter

3 garlic cloves

Sprig of thyme

For lamb belly

2 lamb bellies

Pinch of salt

Pinch of curry powder

For the aubergine purée

4 aubergine

2 tbsp cumin

1 tbsp curry powder

5-6 sprigs of thyme

250ml double cream

4 garlic cloves, crushed

Pinch of salt

For the garlic foam

3 garlic bulbs

250ml cream

250ml whole milk

1 tsp lecithin powder (available from health food shops and online)

For the pommes purée

3kg chippers potatoes

250g butter

250ml double cream

Salt to season

Method

For the lamb loin.

Sear the lamb in a pan with oil on a high heat to get a quick colour and season with Maldon salt. Put on a tray with some butter, garlic and thyme.

Roast the lamb in the oven at 100°c until it reaches 52°c in the middle then allow to rest.

For the confit belly.

Press the two lamb bellies together, sprinkle with salt and curry powder then steam, preferably in a vacuum pac bag or rolled in cling film and steam for 12 hours. When cooked press between two trays with a weight on top and leave until cold. Portion then pan fry the belly until golden on each side.

For the aubergine purée.

Halve three of the aubergines and score then sprinkle with the curry powder, cumin, salt, crushed garlic cloves, sprigs of thyme then wrap in tin foil and roast at 180°c for 40 minutes.

Meanwhile gently heat the cream in a saucepan until lukewarm.

Blitz the roasted aubergine in a blender and add in the cream slowly until it just starts to spin around in the blender and pass through a chinois or a fine sieve then season.

For the aubergine pieces.

Slice the last aubergine into 1cm slices. Trim into a square, score and pan fry with oil until golden on both sides. When golden add butter and thyme to the frying pan for a further 30 seconds then remove and season.

For the garlic foam.

Roast the garlic bulbs at 180°c for 30 minutes. Mash them in a saucepan then pour in the milk and cream. Gently heat to 75°c.

Pass through a chinois or fine sieve then add in the lecithin powder (this stabilises the foam) and hand blitz to create a foam.

For the pommes purée.

Bake the potatoes in the oven at 180°c for 2 hours.

Halve the potatoes then scoop out the inside and pass the scooped out potato through a drum sieve, or potato ricer.

When you have 2kg potatoes add into a large saucepan.

Beat in 250g butter, a knob at time and 250ml warm cream, adding a little bit at a time whilst continuously beating until you have a nice smooth pommes purée. Season to taste.

To serve.

Pipe the aubergine purée on the plate, next to this pipe the pommes purée then slice the lamb loin in to portions and arrange on the plate. Add the aubergine pieces and lamb belly then finish with the garlic foam.

Lobster with laksa sauce beetroot and orange gel

Serves 12.

Ingredients

6 whole lobsters
500g butter
To cook the lobster
1 tail
1 claw
Knob of butter
½ lemon, juiced
Vegetable oil, for frying
Maldon sea salt, to season
Laksa sauce
1 fennel
1 whole chilli
3 lemongrass stalks
1½ shallots
1 tomato
25g ginger
50g macadamia nuts
3 garlic cloves
1 tin coconut milk
2 litres lobster stock
10 kaffir lime leaves
1 tsp fennel seeds
1 tsp curry powder
1 tsp garam masala
100g coriander
Salt, to season
For the beetroots and orange gel
6 golden beetroots
6 raw candied beetroots
For the pickle
500ml white wine vinegar
500g sugar
3 cloves
6 peppercorns
6 coriander seeds
6 fennel seeds
6 white peppercorns
2 sprigs of thyme
1 bay leaf
1 garlic clove
For the orange gel
4 oranges
For every 500ml of juice, you will need
6g agar agar

Method

For the lobster.

Use a chopping board with a cloth underneath for safety. You will need a large cook's knife. Have your boiling water and container of ice water ready before starting this process. Kill the lobster by forcing the knife through the head, pulling it down until the heel hits the board and goes right through the lobster. Twist off the claws into a tray then twist off the tails. Blanch in boiling water for 12 seconds then straight into iced water.

Put the claws in a water bath at 50°c for one hour. After one hour take out the claws one at a time and break the shell using the back of your cook's knife. Pull out the claw in one piece, put into a J-cloth and allow it to dry completely so it's not full of water when you come to vacuum pack it.

Using a pair of scissors, cut down the lobster tails and snap the shells back to release the tail. Pull it out in one piece and lay on a tray with a J-cloth. Take out its waste pipe then the coral. Vacuum pack the coral down for later to make butters or dressings.

Vacuum pack the claws and the tails. Pull out the legs and clean the heads in the sink.

To cook the lobster.

To cook the lobster tail bring to room temperature. Take a medium frying pan with oil and heat on a medium heat. Place the tail on its back, season with a good helping of Maldon sea salt and fry until you have a deep roasted red colour. Turn over and add in the butter and a squeeze of lemon juice. Place in the butter bath at 45°c for 10 minutes. Take out, slice and serve as you see in the picture.

For the laksa sauce.

Peel and thinly chop the shallots, garlic and ginger. Chop and add the fennel, chilli and lemongrass and sweat all of this down until cooked. Season with a little salt. Chop the tomato and add this in. Toast the macadamia nuts then add in with all the dried spices and cook out for a few minutes. Add the coconut milk and lobster stock then bring to a simmer. Blitz in a blender and pass. Then infuse the coriander and kaffir lime leaves in the mixture for 30 minutes and pass through a fine sieve.

For the pickle.

Add all of the ingredients in a pan and bring to the boil for 4 minutes to just thicken the pickle. Once cool pass through a chinois or fine sieve.

Slice the raw candied beetroots thinly, cut out the golden beetroots into discs and keep them covered in lemon water. Wash and vacuum pack the beetroots with a little salt. Steam at 100°c for 40 minutes. Cool down and keep these in the cold pickling liquid.

For the orange gel.

Zest the oranges and in a separate container squeeze in the juice. Blanch the peelings in water for 2 minutes and then put into ice water. Repeat this process 4 times. This is important as it gets rid of a lot of the bitterness.

Add the peelings to the juice and blitz until smooth. Add the orange into a pan with the agar agar. Bring to the boil continuously whisking and allow to set at room temperature. Once set, blitz again in a blender until smooth, and pass through a sieve again, ready to go in a purée bottle.

To serve with lobster.

Spoon the laksa onto a plate and add the lobster. Arrange beetroot slices on and around the lobster as per the picture and add three generous dots of orange gel.

Pressed pork belly, black pudding and peach

This was one of the first dishes that truly represented our philosophy here in the restaurant and we quickly discovered that breeding, rearing, slaughtering and preparing our own pigs is an extremely rewarding experience. We use the pig's blood to make our black pudding and finishing the dish off with the ripest and juiciest peaches that have been simply marinated in a beautiful sherry showcases a range of different textures and temperatures, resulting in a very tasty dish. Serves 4.

Ingredients

For the confit pork belly

½ whole pork belly, bone removed

250g butter

Herb salt to season

Pinch black peppercorns

Pinch coriander seeds

2 star anise

1 cinnamon stick

4 cloves

For the peaches

2 white peaches

1 lime

100ml Pedro Ximénez sherry

100ml vegetable oil

To assemble

Portioned belly pork

160g sliced black pudding

Marinated peaches

Mustard cress, to garnish

Method

For the confit pork belly.

Cut the belly pork in half width-ways and season with all of the spices and the herb salt. Place each half into its own vacuum bag with half of the butter in each one as well. Seal the bag, or wrap in cling film and steam at 85°c overnight.

Once the pork is cooked, remove from the steamer and press in the fridge between 2 baking sheets with weight on the top until completely cold. Once cold, portion into 1 inch cube pieces and return to the fridge until needed.

For the peaches.

Cut the peaches in half and remove the stone. Then cut each half into four, trim to neaten and place into a deep container. Zest and juice the lime and place into a bowl with the sherry and the oil. Using a stick blender blitz until emulsified and pour over the peaches. Leave to marinate.

To assemble.

Preheat the oven to 150°c. Seal the pork in a hot pan on the fat side then place into the oven. Seal the black pudding in the same pan and place in the oven. Roast for 3 minutes until heated thoroughly. Arrange the pork and the black pudding onto a plate with the peaches and dress the plate with mustard cress and a little of the remaining marinade.

Ox cheek pithivier

Braised ox cheek is encased in pastry in this stunning pithivier recipe. Homemade choucroute, which needs to ferment for 15 days before serving, cuts through the richness of the pithivier beautifully. If you don't have the time for this, sauté some finely shredded white cabbage in a pan and add lemon juice and seasoning. Serves 4. Takes 2 weeks for the choucroute.

Ingredients

For the choucroute (part 1)
1kg white cabbage, finely sliced
50g fine sea salt

For the ox cheek
1 pinch fresh thyme, chopped
50g salt
2 ox cheeks

For the vegetables
500ml red wine
75g celery, medium dice
50g onion, medium dice
50g carrots, medium dice
Salt
Pepper
50g leek, medium dice
10ml olive oil

For the shallots
300g shallots
50ml onion oil
Pinch of sea salt, fine
Pinch of thyme
1 pinch black pepper
20g unsalted butter

For the carrots
12 small baby carrots

For the spinach
500g baby spinach leaves
30g butter
Salt

For the pastry
500g puff pastry
1 egg yolk, for egg wash

For the choucroute (part 2)
50g carrots, grated
10ml olive oil
Salt
10g sugar
Pepper

To serve
Baby turnips, washed, leaves on
Handful of baby spinach leaves

Method

First make the choucroute. In a metal bucket, add a layer of cabbage and sprinkle with salt. Using a rolling pin, mash down until watery. Keep repeating this process until all the cabbage has been used.

Leave the cabbage at room temperature for 14 days, then store in the fridge.

For the ox cheeks, start by mixing together the salt and thyme in a bowl until well combined.

To prepare the ox cheeks, remove the top layer of fat and sinew and rub in the thyme salt. Place the cheeks onto a flat grill, grind some pepper onto each side, and fry until a dark golden brown colour.

Preheat the oven to 100°c.

In a large oven tray or saucepan, lightly fry off the celery, carrots, onion and leek in oil until they begin to colour. Add the red wine and the ox cheeks. Boil until the alcohol cooks off and top up with enough water to cover the cheeks. Cook in the oven for 1 hour 30 minutes. After this time, increase the heat to 140°c and cook for a further 2 hours. Remove from the oven and leave on the side to cool for 1 hour. Remove the cheeks from the stock, wrap in cling film and store in the fridge.

Strain the liquid from the pan through a fine strainer into a medium saucepan. Bring to a gentle boil and reduce by three quarters. Season to taste and set aside until ready to serve as a braise reduction.

For the roasted shallots, add the oil, salt and pepper to a pan. Halve the shallots lengthways and place on top of the oil mix, cut-side down. Caramelise the shallots on a very high heat until golden brown, then add the butter and thyme, cover with a cartouche (a disc cut from a sheet of greaseproof paper) and cook until soft on a gentle heat. Remove from the heat and store in the fridge until required.

For the carrots, peel and half lengthways. Blanch in salted boiling water until tender, approximately 3-4 minutes, then strain, refresh in iced water and set aside.

For the spinach, add the butter to a pan over a medium heat. Once foaming, add the baby spinach and cook for approximately 1 minute – until just wilted. Season with salt, remove from the pan and store on a tray lined generously with kitchen towel – this will absorb any excess water.

Before constructing the pithiviers, remove the cheeks from the fridge and use your hands to break the meat down into small flaked chunks.

Roll out the pastry to 4mm thickness and then leave to rest in the fridge for 45 minutes.

Lay out the pastry sheet and cut out 8 circles of pastry, 5 inches in diameter each.

Brush egg wash over 4 of the pastry bases. On each base, layer on the flaked ox cheek, the caramelised carrots, wilted spinach, some more ox cheek and the roasted shallots.

Lay the remaining circles of pastry on top, then smooth down on top of the filling, taking care not to tear the pastry. Press the edges of the top circle onto the edges of the base to seal each pithivier.

Brush the pithiviers all over with egg wash and leave in the fridge for 10 minutes.

Remove from the fridge, take a knife and starting at the top in the centre, score half circles down the sides, being careful not to pierce all the way through the pastry.

Where the edges meet, make a seal at the bottom and use a knife to score lines 1cm apart all the way around the base. Rest for a further 20 minutes in the fridge.

Preheat the oven to 180°c.

Remove the pithiviers from the fridge and bake in the oven for 20 minutes until golden brown.

Meanwhile, measure out 100g of choucroute per person and squeeze out the excess liquid. Mix with the carrot, onion, olive oil, sugar and salt and pepper to taste.

Before assembling the final dish, reheat the braise reduction in a small pan and set aside.

Remove the pithiviers from the oven and place into the middle of each plate. Place a quenelle of the choucroute alongside followed by some baby spinach leaves and turnips. Drizzle over 2-3 tablespoons of the braise reduction and serve immediately.

Squab pigeon

Serves 4.

Ingredients

4 squab pigeons

4 garlic cloves

4 sprigs of thyme

1 tsp herb salt

150g butter

For the salt crust pastry

600g salt

1kg flour

400ml water

7 egg whites

Egg wash

For the confit pigeon legs

Pigeon legs, from the squabs

Herb salt

Large knob of butter

Method

Chop the head off the squab and take off the wings and legs. Keep the legs to confit them. Keep the wings for sauce.

Take out the insides and stuff with garlic and thyme.

In a frying pan roast the bird, caramelising the skin on a medium heat. Don't take too long, otherwise you will start to cook the pigeon. Once golden all of the way around take off the heat and chill in the fridge.

To make the salt crust pastry, combine all the ingredients in a large bowl and mix well.

Wrap the squab in the salt crust pastry then use a pastry cutter to make the wings and form a head as per picture. The pastry around the pigeon should be half a centimetre thick.

Egg wash and then cook at 220°c for around 10 minutes, or until the centre reaches 52°c.

Rest for 5 minutes then break the salt crust and carve the bird.

For the confit pigeon legs.

Season the legs with herb salt. Wrap with the butter in cling film and cook in a pan of water at 70°c overnight. Alternatively vacuum pack and cook in a water bath or steamer.

Duck and pistachio

Serves 4.

Ingredients

1 large whole duck

500g pistachios, peeled and unsalted

500g English black cherries

1 litre duck fat, ask your butcher

3 cardamom pods

3 juniper berries

3 cloves

3 tsp thyme, finely chopped

3 garlic cloves, crushed

3 bay leaves

1 tbsp lovage, finely chopped

Salt & pepper to season

For the rillette

1kg chippers potatoes

100g butter, cubed

100ml cream

100g Parmesan, grated

3 eggs, beaten

200g plain flour

200g breadcrumbs

Salt & pepper to season

Method

To make the rillette, wash and bake the potatoes whole at 180°c for 1 hour 30 minutes.

Remove from oven, halve the potatoes and leave to cool for 5 minutes. You want them to still be warm when you use them. Scoop out the potato flesh and pass through a fine sieve, alternatively you can mash.

In a pan place the sieved potatoes on a medium heat, add the butter slowly in cubes, and beat it through the potato using a wooden spoon. Then slowly add the cream whilst continually beating and then add the Parmesan.

Season with salt and pepper to taste, you could also chop some fresh herbs like chives, lovage or parsley for an extra dimension.

Roll in to sausage shapes and place in the fridge for 2 hours.

When chilled roll them in the flour, tap off any excess, then roll in the egg, then roll through the breadcrumbs. Place back in the fridge until you are ready to deep fry at 180°c for 2 minutes then serve.

For the duck.

Add the duck fat to a saucepan with the cardamom, juniper berries, cloves, thyme, garlic and bay leaves and bring the fat up to 90°c. Remove the legs, season them with sea salt and place them in the duck fat and leave at 90°c for 2 hours to confit.

Remove from the fat, take off the skin then pick the meat from the bone and place in a bowl. Season with salt and pepper.

Add 50ml of the cooled duck fat back in to the meat and mix and gently fold in the chopped lovage.

Lay out a strip of cling film, giving yourself a metre to play with. Place the confit duck leg meat in the middle of the cling film ready to roll into a sausage shape. Wrap the cling film and twist at the ends to make a solid and tight duck leg roll. Place in the fridge for 1 hour to cool.

To serve slice into portions, remove the cling film and fry the ends.

Remove the breasts from the duck, season the skin with salt and pepper and then fry it in a saucepan at a low heat, skin side down, so that the fat comes out of the skin.

Place your pan in the oven at 120°c for 10-12 minutes (this is for very pink but stay calm you will rest it for 15 minutes which will allow the blood to come out of the meat, so it will not look raw, and the meat will be very tender).

For the pistachio purée.

This can be done the day before. Place the pistachios on an oven tray, season with a little salt and then bake for approximately 5 minutes until golden at 180°c.

Place them in a blender until smooth using a little duck fat to create a purée.

Dice up your cherries roughly and then plate up your dish just like the picture.

Sea trout and pea fricassee

Serves 2.

Ingredients

For the pickled onions

30g baby silverskin onions

500ml white wine vinegar

500g sugar

3 cloves

6 peppercorns

6 coriander seeds

6 fennel seeds

6 white peppercorns

2 sprigs of thyme

1 bay leaf

1 garlic clove

For the sea trout

2 x 150g trout fillets, pin-boned

Baking parchment

Lemon juice

2 knobs of butter

Salt, to season

Vegetable oil, for frying

For the pea fricassee

100g petit pois

100g tomato

30g pickled onions (see below)

30g shallots

½ lemon, juiced

3g salt

Method

For the pickled onions.

Add all of the ingredients, except the onions, in a pan and bring to the boil for 4 minutes to thicken slightly. Add in the onions whilst hot and leave for two hours.

For the sea trout.

Place the parchment in a frying pan and drizzle in the vegetable oil. Heat the pan up to a medium heat, season the trout fillet and place skin side down. Press down to make sure you keep the skin nice and flat. As it fries, the skin goes nice and crispy, adding a another texture to the dish.

Once the fish is cooked 80 percent of the way through, turn over and add a squeeze of lemon juice and the butter. Finish in the oven at 140°c for 1 and a half minutes.

For the pea fricassee.

Blanch and peel the tomatoes. Halve them, take out the hearts and brunoise (very finely diced) the petals. Peel and brunoise the shallots and sweat them down in a pan. In the same pan add the tomatoes, petis pois, pickled onions, lemon and salt. Cook quickly to heat up.

Ginger panna cotta with poached rhubarb lemon cream and rhubarb sorbet

Serves 8.

Ingredients

For the ginger panna cotta

750ml cream

120g ginger sugar (jar of stem ginger)

3 gelatine leaves

For the pâte sablé

500g plain flour

200g butter

150g icing or caster sugar

1 vanilla pod

2 eggs

1 lemon, zest

For the rhubarb sorbet

1 litre rhubarb purée

1 litre strawberry purée

1 litre water

500g sugar

For the ganache

300g white chocolate

400ml cream

For the lemon curd

315ml fresh lemon juice

6 eggs

240g butter, cubed

140g sugar

For the poached rhubarb

5 sticks rhubarb

500ml strawberry purée

100g sugar

200ml water

Method

For the ginger panna cotta.

For the ginger sugar, buy one jar and blitz in a blender until smooth.

Soak your gelatine in water.

Heat up the cream and add in the sugar. Once it comes to the boil whisk in the gelatine. Set in a mould, preferably a dome shaped one like in the picture.

For the pâte sablé.

Preheat the oven to 180°c. With a mixer use the paddle attachment and cream together the butter and sugar. Add the inside of the vanilla pod and the lemon zest. Add in the flour and 2 eggs (at room temperature).

Once it comes together take out, cling film leave to set in the fridge.

Roll out to ½cm thick then cut out the same size bases of your panna cotta. Bake at 180°c for 7 minutes.

Allow to cool then put your panna cotta on top.

For the rhubarb sorbet.

Bring the water and the sugar to boil and add in the purées. Take off the heat, hand blitz and then churn in an ice cream maker or place in a container and freeze in the fridge, mixing with a fork every hour.

For the ganache.

Bring the cream to the boil and pour over the chocolate. Leave for a few minutes and whisk in to make a ganache.

For the lemon curd.

In a bowl over a pan of hot water (a bain-marie) whisk the sugar, lemon juice and eggs over the heat until they thicken then cool down to 40°c. Hand blitz in the butter cubes and chill.

Then whisk together 300g ganache with 150g of lemon curd until it makes a thick mousse.

For the poached rhubarb.

Peel the rhubarb. Mix together the strawberry purée, water and sugar vacuum pack with the rhubarb. Steam at 100°c for 8 minutes. Alternatively, just poach in the strawberry liquor for 8 minutes.

Bex McGurran's Tiffin

This is one of the first recipes I learnt from my mother and one of the first recipes I made with my children as it's so easy to do and you can also change the ingredients to your own tastes.

Serves 8.

Ingredients

150g butter

150g dark chocolate

2 tbsp golden syrup

150g broken Rich Tea biscuits

120g broken Digestive biscuits (swap these for ginger nuts at Christmas)

Optional additions

Pinch of sea salt (Colin's addition!)

Grated orange (Christmas)

Grated lime (summer)

Chopped glacier cherries (for my Mum in law!)

Homemade honeycomb (My Mummy's addition and great for a hiking snack)

Method

This recipe is one that you can do with the children.

Slowly melt the butter and chocolate together into a big bowl. Short bursts in the microwave of 30 seconds with a lot of stirring in between times. Once nice and smooth add the golden syrup and stir until mixed well, at this point add your seasonal ingredients. Then add the biscuits and stir through so everything is covered with chocolate.

I use a round cake tin and line it with baking parchment so it's easy to deal with but you can use a loaf tin or any shape container you like.

Pack the mix into the tin then place a weight on top and put in the fridge for 1 hour 30 minutes.

If for a special occasion decorate with icing sugar and cocoa or cover in chocolate swirls.

About
The Family

Would you like a little more tea?

One of the most remarkable things that has happened over the ten years at Winteringham Fields is the extension of our own family. The way we work means that the McGurran family is much more than me, Bex and our girls Olivia, Emily and Jessica.

Each January we close the restaurant and head off to France on a skiing holiday. All of the team and their partners are invited, making it an annual highlight for everybody. The chalet has had to get larger over the years but it means we have a great time year upon year.

Winteringham is such a special place; it would be hard not to make friends. Through working the fields we have got to know the local farmers as they have passed on their knowledge and expertise. The restaurant and outbuildings are large and meandering, so it seems barely a day goes by when there's not a plumber, electrician, painter, decorator or delivery driver knocking around. All of these people have become a part of our lives, making Winteringham an extraordinary place to work.

Each summer we throw a barbecue, which was initially a way of thanking the staff for their hard work, friendship and help in hours of need. Naturally, it has since escalated and has become something of a family day for the extended WF family; from ex-staff to plumbers with children thrown in for good measure, it's a great day and one hell of a clean-up. A mad hatter's tea party of epic proportions…

Summer

Winteringham is in full production and farmers are making the most of the long hours of daylight before the nights start drawing in. It's a magical time in the village which exhibits the sounds, smells and colours of the countryside at its best. It's this time of year that Winteringham really shines.

Our work continues on the land and we experiment with the crops further. We might let some rocket run to seed to find out whether the flower heads can add an extra element to a dish, imagining the creative possibilities wherever possible.

While many of our customers are abroad on their summer holidays we start planning the Christmas menu, getting the message out there to our loyal customers via social media and mailing lists. While it seems unnatural to think about Christmas in August, you've got to plan ahead so you don't fall behind.

Summer 2015 marked our tenth anniversary here at Winteringham Fields, which gave us time to reflect on the journey we have taken and wonder which road we will follow next. We're not ones to sit still and are always dreaming of another venture to take things down more exciting routes.

But summer is also a time to catch our breath. We close for two and half weeks, taking a well-earned family holiday.

Eggs benedict

Ingredients

1 breakfast muffin

4 eggs

200g clarified butter

1 tsp white wine vinegar

Salt

Pepper

Chives

2 slices good quality Parma ham

Method

Slice the breakfast muffins in half and toast. Place the Parma ham on top.

Poach two eggs for 3 minutes and serve directly seasoning with salt, pepper

To make the hollandaise, put two egg yolks and the vinegar in a bowl, sit on top of boiling water and whisk until the eggs become light and fluffy. Slowly pour in the butter whilst continually whisking until you have a thick sauce consistency.

Pour the sauce on top of the eggs and place under the grill to caramelise the sauce a little bit. Finish with a sprinkle of chives.

Smoked haddock chowder
with crispy potato poached egg

❦❧❦

Serves 8-10.

Ingredients

For the poached eggs

10 hen eggs

5 litres water

Splash of white wine vinegar

For the potato spaghetti

2 large chipper potatoes

Oil, for deep frying

For the smoked haddock

1 smoked haddock

Butter, for frying

½ lemon, juiced

For the onion and smoked haddock purée

4 white onions, chopped

200g haddock

100g butter

100ml cream

100g celery

Celery leaves

Method

For the poached eggs.

In a pan bring the water and vinegar to the boil. Crack the eggs into the boiling water, one by one and cook for 2-3 minutes. Once cooked remove the eggs from the pan and place them in ice cold water until needed.

For the potato spaghetti.

Peel and wash the potatoes, then using a mandoline or spiraliser slice into spaghetti. Blanch the potato spaghetti in boiling water for 5 seconds then place in a bowl of ice cold water. Using the poached eggs as the centre and wrap your potato spaghetti around the eggs, making sure you cover the whole egg. When you are ready to serve, deep fry for 2 minutes.

For the smoked haddock.

Firstly remove the pin bones from the fish then remove the skin and portion as you would like. It is best to pan fry this last with butter and lemon juice until golden brown.

For the onion and smoked haddock purée.

Sweat the onions in butter and cover with cling film until soft but not coloured. Add the smoked haddock to the onions then cook for 5 minutes. Once the 5 minutes are up, strain the mixture to remove the butter but keep the onion juices for the purée. Using a blender blitz the onion with hot cream until smooth, then pass through a sieve.

Peel and finely dice the celery, but keep the small leaves as they can be used to garnish the dish.

Full English breakfast

*I thought I would have to put our full English breakfast in our book as this was the catalyst
for our whole philosophy of rearing all our produce for the restaurant. We started off with having
chickens for the fried eggs, then moved onto rearing pigs for the bacon, sausages and black pudding,
before growing our own plump tomatoes and finally caramelising apples from our many trees on the
grounds behind the kitchen. This really sums up all of the collective hardwork and effort that goes into
creating one dish. It's all about the very good quality produce for a classic hearty breakfast that we all
deserve to indulge in at times. Serves 1.*

Ingredients

1 sausage

2 rashers bacon

1 piece black pudding

½ large plum tomato

Granny Smith apple, cored and sliced

1 egg

3 button mushrooms

2 knobs butter

Demerara sugar

Method

On a tray, oil and season the sausage. Grill until evenly golden all the way
around. Probe it, and once it reaches 70°c in the middle, serve.

Grill the bacon until the fat on the outside just starts to caramelise.

Reheat the black pudding under the grill.

Sprinkle the apple with Demerara sugar and grill until the sugar caramelises
and the apple is soft.

Quarter the mushrooms, heat a frying pan with some oil and fry until
golden all over. Season and add in a knob of butter, then serve.

Grill the tomato with a knob of butter on top and season.

Crack the egg in the same frying pan from the mushrooms and fry.

Pestle and mortar

This makes 4 mortars.

Ingredients

12 lovage leaves

12 mint leaves

100ml liquid nitrogen

For the 20 meringues

50g egg whites

100g caster sugar

For the natural yoghurt sorbet

100ml milk

100ml cream

12g cornflour

75g caster sugar

50ml water

500ml natural yoghurt

¼ lemon juice

Method

For the meringues.

Whisk the egg whites and sugar in a bowl and mix over a pan of hot water until the sugar is dissolved and the egg whites are smooth, not grainy, to the touch. Whisk in a stand mixer or with an electric hand whisk until a soft peak meringue is formed. Pipe into 5 pence sized meringues, and then dry at 70°c for a minimum of 4 hours.

For the natural yoghurt sorbet.

Mix all the ingredients together apart from the yoghurt, lemon juice and liquid nitrogen. Bring to the boil whilst continuously whisking and pour in the yoghurt and lemon juice. Cool down and pour into an ice cream churner. Churn until frozen then place in a freezer container and freeze until set. If you do not have an ice cream maker then put the mix into a container in the frezzer and whisk every hour to keep it smooth before use.

Add 3 leaves of lovage and 3 leaves of the mint in each mortar with 5 meringues. Pour in liquid nitrogen to quick freeze the herbs (if nitrogen is unavailable pre-freeze the herbs and meringue, and place in the mortar last minute). Use a pestle quickly to pound into a fine powder. Add a quenelle of the yoghurt sorbet and move it around the herb mixture to coat it thoroughly. Bon appetit!

Smoked salmon scrambled egg

Serves 1.

Ingredients

3 whole eggs

15g unsalted butter

50g smoked salmon

Salt & pepper to season

1 breakfast muffin

Watercress, for garnish

Method

Slice half of the smoked salmon into bite-sized pieces and roll the other half into a rose shape for presentation later. Crack all the eggs in a heavy-based pan with the butter and seasoning. Place on a medium heat and stir until the mixture is nearly cooked. Remove from the heat and add the chopped smoked salmon. Let the residual heat left in the pan finish cooking the eggs.

To serve, place onto buttered toasted muffins and top with the smoked salmon rose and watercress, or pea shoots.

Beef tartare

Serves 8.

Ingredients

250g aged beef fillet

1 lemon, juice only

100ml white truffle oil

1 tbsp Worcestershire sauce

Salt and freshly ground black pepper

1 tbsp Dijon mustard

1 shallot, very finely chopped

25g flat leaf parsley, finely chopped

10g chives, finely chopped

8 sheets rice paper

To serve

Ponzu gel

Method

Mince the beef fillet in a mincer with a medium sized mincing plate, or ask your butcher to do this for you. Place into a bowl and add all the other ingredients apart from the rice paper. Place in the fridge to chill for about 8 hours, or preferably overnight.

Once rested, roll into 12g balls and place back into the fridge to firm up.

Prepare the rice paper by soaking it in hot water for 5 seconds to soften, lay onto a well-oiled surface and with a round cutter, cut 3 circles and place a ball of tartare into the middle. Then wrap in the rice paper and repeat until all balls are wrapped. Then place in the fridge until you are ready to serve.

To serve, remove from the fridge and arrange on a platter.

Serve with a ponzu gel.

Suckling pig, leek, pickled onion and hummus

Serves 6.

Ingredients

For the suckling pig

1 suckling pig loin

1.5kg suckling pig leg meat

150g smoked bacon

250ml reduced pork stock

6 savoy cabbage leaves

2 suckling pig bellies

Herbs and salts, to season

For the hummus

400g chickpeas

3 garlic cloves

175ml hot water

75ml olive oil

1 tsp smoked paprika

Pinch salt

Lemon juice

2 tsp sugar

125g tahini

1 tsp cumin

For the pickled onions

250ml water

250ml white wine vinegar

250g sugar

500g silverskin onions

6 black peppercorns

2 star anise

6 cloves

4 bay leaves

Method

For the suckling pig.

Trim the suckling pig loin of all of the sinew, portion into 40g portions and vacuum pack or wrap in cling film. Mince the leg meat with the smoked bacon and combine with the stock. Season to taste and place in the fridge to set. Once set, roll into 40g balls and place back into the fridge. Blanch the cabbage leaves for 2 minutes then lay onto cling film squares. Place a pork ball in the middle then wrap the cabbage around to form a ball.

Bone out both of the bellies and season well with herbs and salts. Place flesh to flesh and vacuum pack in a large bag, or wrap tightly in cling film. At 85°c, steam overnight. Once cooked press between two baking sheets with a weight on top and put in the fridge until completely cold. Once cold, remove the skin and portion into 1cm by 5cm long pieces.

For the hummus.

Place all ingredients into a blender and whizz until very smooth then season to taste.

For the pickled onions.

Place the water, vinegar, sugar, peppercorns, star anise, cloves and bay leaves in a pan and bring to the boil. Once the sugar has dissolved, take off the stove. Halve the onions and pour the hot pickle mixture over them, then leave to cool. Once cool peel the onions and place back into the pickle and put in the fridge. (Continued...)

Suckling pig, leek, pickled onion and hummus (continued)

Serves 6.

Ingredients

For the steamed leeks

6 leeks

100g butter

Pinch salt

For the chickpea fricassee

100g chickpeas

500g silverskin onions

1 shallot

1 garlic clove

10g chives

1 lemon juice

Pinch salt

10g butter

For the pig crackling

20g large air bag pig skin

Herb salt

Oil, for deep frying

For the sauce

Bones from suckling

5 litres chicken stock

500g carrots

500g onions

2 sticks celery

1 leek, trimmed

1 bulb garlic

25g thyme

150g tomato purée

1 bottle red wine

250g cold butter, cubed

Method

For the steamed leeks.

Wash and trim the leeks, leaving them whole. Place into a large vacuum pack bag, or wrap in cling film, with the butter and salt and steam at 100°c for 30 minutes. Leave to go cold, slice into 1 inch pieces and leave to one side.

For the chickpea fricassee.

Finely chop the shallot and garlic and cook in the butter until soft but not coloured. Add the whole silverskin onions and chickpeas and continue to cook for 2 minutes, but make sure they do not colour. Finish with lemon, salt and chives.

For the pig crackling.

Deep fry the air bag at 190°c until puffed up and crispy. Whilst still hot, season with the herb salt.

For the sauce.

Roast the bones for 1 hour at 180°c until dark in colour. In a large stock pot colour the vegetables, garlic and thyme until dark then add the tomato purée. Cook out the purée for five minutes then add the stock and suckling bones. Bring to a simmer and cook for 12 hours, pass through a muslin cloth 3 times into a clean pan. Add the wine, bring to the boil and reduce by two thirds until thick and flavoursome. Whilst boiling whisk in the butter to enrich.

To finish, place the loin in a water bath at 55°c for 30 minutes, or poach in hot water. Cook the cabbage ball at 120°c for 10 minutes. Seal the belly on both sides and place into a tray of simmer sauce along with the other meat.

On the plate swipe the hummus, place the fricassee on top and then the crispy skin on top of that. Arrange the meat in a line with the leeks either side and drizzle the sauce to cover.

Roast chicken

Dry chicken is always a problem, as such I cook mine at a low temperature and go against the usual rule of thumb of resting for half the cooking time; this results in a moist, tender and juicy roast. If the bird is cooked too hot that is when you end up with the dreaded dry chicken that we have all experienced! Serves 4.

Ingredients

1 whole chicken

1 tsp paprika

1 tbsp butter, at room temperature

1 tbsp Maldon salt

Pinch of black pepper

8 sprigs of thyme

4 garlic cloves, peeled and crushed

Stock cube (optional)

Method

Preheat the oven to 120°c.

Place the chicken in a large roasting tin and rub the paprika, butter, salt and pepper all over the skin. Add the thyme and garlic to the roasting tin with the chicken or perhaps crumble a stock cube over the skin.

Roast the chicken in the oven for approximately 1 hour and 20-30 minutes (the centre of the meat should reach 48°c if you have a temperature probe). Remove from the oven, cover with tin foil and allow to rest for 30 minutes on top of the stove before serving.

Carve and serve with your roast accompaniments of choice.

Mel's salmon with Parma ham, spicy cabbage salad and hasselback potatoes

It is really an honour to have our friend Mel appear in this book as we are often around at each other's houses entertaining with music, drink and wonderful food. Together with his wife Anna they can produce the most soul nourishing food that we all like to enjoy next to their cosy fire. Every time we go I always come back having eaten something that I've never tried before, with Anna being Swedish, and both having spent a considerable portion of their life together at sea visiting many different countries, I think their tastes are possibly more eclectic than mine! They create the most interesting dishes pairing the most unusual ingredients. The inspiration they provide along with their valued friendship is something I look forward to for many more years ahead. Serves 4.

Ingredients

4 salmon steaks, skin on

Fresh tarragon

4 slices Parma ham

1 sweetheart cabbage

2 limes

2 red chillies

1 bunch fresh coriander

1 tbsp sugar

8 medium sized potatoes

Handful pomegranate seeds

Sea salt

Olive oil

Method

For the salad, remove outer leaves and finely chop the cabbage before placing into a bowl. De-seed and chop the chillies and add to the bowl. Chop the coriander and add to the bowl. Sprinkle over sugar and squeeze the juice from the limes into the bowl. Add the pomegranate seeds, give the whole salad a good stir, cover with cling film and leave to stand for one hour, stirring occasionally.

Without peeling, slice the potatoes thinly, but not all the way through. Place the potatoes in a roasting tin with the sliced side up. Drizzle liberally with olive oil and sprinkle with sea salt. Bake at 225°c for approximately 45 minutes, until cooked and golden brown.

For the fish, finely chop the tarragon and place on the top of the salmon. Sprinkle on a little sea salt and then place the Parma ham over the salmon (but not on the skin side) and place in tin foil. Barbecue the salmon on a medium heat until cooked and golden brown.

Serve the salmon on a bed of the cabbage salad with the hasselback potatoes and enjoy!

Jane Warburton's
sloe gin or damson vodka

This recipe can be used for both sloe gin or damson vodka, ideal for the fruit you have to hand. Damsons left over after the vodka is strained are delicious to eat with ice cream or yogurt.

This makes a perfect Christmas gift. Make a few months in advance and tie with a ribbon or deliver in a festive box. You could even present it with some homemade cheese crackers, or chocolate truffles. Makes about 800ml.

Ingredients

450g sloes or damsons

750ml vodka or gin

350g caster sugar

Method

Remove the stems from the fruit and prick with a fork to break their skins. If you're doing a large batch, freeze overnight to break the skins instead.

Place the fruit in a large, sterilised preserving jar with the alcohol and sugar. (You can sterilise your jars in a very hot dishwasher, or boil in a pan of water for 10 minutes.)

If you prefer a more tart drink then add less sugar (250g). You can always add more if it is too tart at the re-bottling stage, once you have tasted the drink.

Close the jar tightly and store in a cool, dark place for 2-3 months, ideally turning it every few days until the sugar dissolves.

To bottle, strain the liquid and pour into warm, dry, sterilised bottles.

Seal, label and date. The contents will keep for many years.

Octopus

Serves 4.

Ingredients

1 whole octopus, frozen and thawed
our
200ml dashi stock

For the orange gel

2 whole oranges

200ml orange juice

6g agar agar

20g sugar

For the prawn dill mix

100g fresh prawns

10g dill, chopped

20g crème fraîche

Salt & pepper to season

Method

For the octopus.

Place thawed octopus in vacuum pac bag or wrap tightly in cling film, with the dashi stock and simmer in hot water for 3 hours.

Remove and cool to room temperature.

Once cool enough to handle, hold the tentacles in one hand and slice off the head just above the tentacles. Push the beak off with your thumb.

Reserve the tentacles in the warm dashi stock.

Lay out sheets of cling film on your work surface to cover an area about one metre long and 50cm wide and layer 2-3 times on top of each other.

Lay out the tentacles in a bunch on the cling film and then roll the tentacles tightly in the cling film. Tie each end until the wrapped octopus is sausage like, being about 4 inches thick.

Freeze the wrapped octopus overnight.

For the orange gel.

Peel the oranges and squeeze the juice into a bowl, be sure to remove as much of the white pith from the skin as possible. Reserve the orange peel.

Bring a pan of orange juice to the boil and have a bowl of ice water ready at the side.

Blanch the peelings in the juice for 30 seconds and then plunge into the ice water, repeat this 3 times.

Mix together the juice from the oranges and the orange juice and add the blanched peelings. Add the sugar and agar agar.

Transfer to a powerful blender and blend until smooth.

Pour into a flat tray and leave to set. Once cold blend again in a food blender and keep in a squeezy bottle until needed.

For the prawn mix.

Lightly fry the prawns in a warm pan.

Add the chopped dill and then transfer to a bowl.

Once mixture is cool, season with salt and pepper and then add crème fraîche.

To serve.

Remove the octopus from the freezer and using a meat slicer or very sharp knife slice 5 good slices per portion about 3mm thick. Remove the cling film, arrange onto a plate in a ring and allow to defrost.

Squeeze a few dots of the orange gel around the octopus and quenelle a good helping of prawn mix into the centre of the octopus ring.

Vanilla rice pudding
with poached rhubarb

Ingredients

For the rice pudding

500ml whole milk

500ml double cream

135g caster sugar

180g pudding rice

1 vanilla pod, split and seeds scraped

2 large egg yolks

For the poached rhubarb

500g fresh rhubarb

150g strawberry purée

75ml water

75g caster sugar

Method

Put the milk, cream and 90g of the sugar into a heavy-based saucepan and stir over a low heat until the sugar has dissolved. Bring to the boil and immediately reduce the heat to a simmer. Tip in the rice and the vanilla, and simmer very slowly for 45 minutes to 1 hour until the rice is tender. Give the mixture a stir every so often to prevent the rice from catching and burning to the bottom of the pan. Remove from the heat and take out the vanilla pod, cover with cling film directly onto the rice pudding and leave for 15-20 minutes.

Meanwhile whisk the remaining sugar and yolks until white and fluffy. Fold this through the rice pudding and if serving warm, serve immediately. If serving cold allow to cool completely and fold through a little cream to loosen.

Cut the rhubarb into 1 inch pieces and place into a large vacuum pac bag, alternatively wrap tightly in cling film.

Mix the other ingredients together and pour into the bag, then steam at 100°c for 8 minutes. Serve on top of the rice pudding.

Baked Alaska

Ingredients

For the Genoise sponge

250g golden caster sugar

8 medium eggs

250g plain flour

50g butter

For the rhubarb and strawberry sorbet

500g rhubarb purée

500g strawberry purée

500ml water

250g sugar

5g sorbet stabiliser (available online)

For the Italian meringue

110g egg whites

30g sugar

100ml water

300g sugar

To serve

Grand Marnier (optional)

Method

Preheat the oven to 180°c. Put the sugar and eggs in a heatproof bowl and sit over a pan of just simmering water. Beat with an electric whisk until hot then remove from the heat and beat continuously for 10 minutes. The mixture will double in volume and should fall in ribbons on the surface when dripped from the whisk. Melt the butter until it starts to turn golden (called a beurre noisette) then with the whisk running add the melted butter. Sieve in the flour and fold very gently into the mixture with a large metal spoon; be careful not to over-mix as this will prevent the cake rising properly. Spread the mixture over a lined greaseproof baking sheet in a thin layer. Bake for 8 minutes.

In a pan bring the water and sugar to the boil to form a stock syrup. Do not reduce once the sugar has dissolved, remove from the heat and add the purées and stabiliser. Place into a container and freeze until ready to serve, whisking every hour to keep soft or churn in an ice cream maker until frozen. Place into the freezer until ready to use.

Make a stock syrup with the 300g sugar and 100ml of water by placing into a pan and bringing to 150°c. Whilst this is on the stove whisk the egg whites and the 30g sugar together until soft peaks are formed. Then pour in the hot stock syrup and keep whisking until the meringue is cool. Place into a piping bag until ready to use.

Assembling the Alaska.

Place the churned sorbet into a half pipe mould, or any mould you desire. Once the sorbet is in the mould replace back into the freezer to firm up again. This will take roughly 12 hours. Once fully set cut your cooled sponge to the size of the base of your chosen mould and turn out onto a suitable serving platter. Now decorate with the Italian meringue, piping with a star nozzle. Now the fun bit! Flambé a pan of Grand Marnier and spoon the flaming liquor over the Alaska in front of your guest. Alternatively you can just blow torch the meringue to a nice golden brown and serve.

Doughnuts with a hot chocolate sauce

Ingredients

250g plain flour

1 tsp salt

25g caster sugar

15g fresh yeast

40ml whole milk

1 large egg, lightly beaten

½ tbsp dark rum

40g butter

Vegetable oil, for deep-frying

For the chocolate sauce

250g dark chocolate, small buttons

75ml water

75g sugar

Method

Place the flour, salt, and sugar in a bowl and using an electric mixer with a dough hook and stir to combine. Make a well in the centre. Place the yeast in the milk and stir until creamy, then add this to the well. Add the egg and rum to the well, then using an electric whisk on a low speed, stir to combine. Gently increase the speed and mix until it comes together to form a ball. Add the butter a little at a time until fully incorporated and the dough is smooth. Place the dough into a lightly greased bowl and cover with cling film. Leave to prove slowly in the fridge overnight, by which time the dough should have doubled in size. Knock back the dough and lightly knead on a floured surface. Shape into 40g sized golf balls, place onto a greased baking tray placed well apart from each other and put in a warm place for 1-2 hours, until they have almost doubled in size.

Place the sugar and water in a pan and bring to the boil until the sugar has dissolved. Whilst the syrup is still hot pour over the chocolate and stir until the chocolate has melted and the sauce is thick, smooth and shiny. Keep warm.

To cook the doughnuts, heat the oil in a deep fat fryer or heavy-based saucepan to 190°c. In small batches deep fry the doughnuts until golden brown all over. Remove from the fryer onto a tray lined with kitchen paper, toss the doughnuts in caster sugar and serve warm with the chocolate sauce.

Olive brioche

Ingredients

250g bread flour

150g whole eggs

30g sugar

11.5g fresh yeast

200g unsalted butter

1 egg yolk

1 tsp salt

100g olives

Method

Mix all the ingredients together, except for the egg yolk and butter, until fully combined together and the dough is smooth.

Cube the butter and leave to reach room temperature (37°c). Then, slowly add the butter one dice at a time – each dice should incorporate into the dough before adding another.

Add the egg yolks until just combined, and then stop mixing. They should be very soft and tacky to the touch. Leave at room temperature to double in size, then knock back and leave in the fridge overnight.

Finely chop the olive in a food processor, roll out the brioche dough until 1cm thick and spread the olive mixture onto it in an even layer.

Roll the whole thing into a Swiss roll and slice into 50g portions. Place into dariole moulds (small dome-shaped moulds) and prove at room temperature until they have doubled in size.

Once fully proved, place in a preheated oven at 180°c for 15 minutes.

To make plain brioche just leave out the olive mixture.

Berry gratin
with Champagne sabayon

❦❧❦

Serves 4.

Ingredients

450g mixed berries (raspberries, strawberries, blackberries, blueberries)

55g caster sugar

2 large egg yolks

125ml double cream, lightly whipped

2-3 tbsp Champagne

Mint leaves, to garnish

Method

Divide the berries between four plates reserving some for decoration.

Put the sugar and yolks into a large heatproof bowl and set the bowl over a pan of barely simmering water.

Using an electric whisk beat the mixture until it is thick and creamy and has tripled in volume. It should be thick enough to leave a ribbon trail on the surface when lifted.

Fold in the cream and Champagne to taste, spoon the mixture over the berries and blow torch quickly until golden.

Scatter with reserved fruit and mint leaves.

Pineapple and basil bomb

Ingredients

1 ripe pineapple

4g basil leaves

For the white chocolate coating

200g white chocolate

200g cocoa butter

To serve

Coconut

Lime zest

Popping candy

Method

Top and tail the pineapple and remove the skin using a knife. Cut into quarters length ways and remove the inner woody stalk running through the middle. Chop the pineapple into one inch pieces and place in a jug blender with the basil leaves. Blitz until smooth and pass through a fine chinois or sieve. Pour the mixture into half sphere moulds and place into the freezer overnight until well frozen.

The next day, remove from the freezer and take two of the half spheres out of the moulds, turn them flat side down and gently rub on a work bench for a few seconds to melt the top layer. Push the two halves together, place back into the mould and once all have been done place the whole tray back into the freezer to ensure they are well frozen. Now prepare the white chocolate coating.

Place both ingredients in a mixing bowl and place over a pan of simmering water. Once the two are melted and combined well, remove from heat. Take the spheres of pineapple and basil out of the freezer, with a pin stab one of the spheres and quickly dip it in the chocolate mixture. Take the pin out and place into a container, repeat this process until all of the bombs are coated and place into a fridge overnight to allow the mixture inside to defrost. To serve, place on a bed of coconut with lime zest and popping candy on top. Eat with caution, prone to explode on contact!

Peaches

Serves 6.

Ingredients

For the parfait

500ml peach purée or juices

200g caster sugar

60ml water

12 egg yolks

500ml double cream

For the honeycomb

80ml honey

160g sugar

8g baking powder

For the fresh peaches

2 yellow peaches

Method

For the parfait.

Bring the sugar and water to 121°c. Whisk with an electric whisk until pale. Pour the hot syrup into the egg yolks in a slow and steady stream and whisk until the mixture goes light and fluffy and cool.

Once cold fold the purée into the egg yolks. Whisk the cream to soft peaks and fold into the mixture. Pour into a mould and level off, then freeze.

For the honeycomb.

Put the honey into a pan first and warm, (as evenly as possible) sprinkle over the sugar. Bring to 115°c, add in the baking powder, and whisk very quickly. Transfer as fast as possible onto a tray with greaseproof paper and put in the fridge or freezer to allow to set. Break up the honeycomb and store in an airtight container.

Halve the yellow peaches and twist to release the stone. Quarter them and serve on top of the parfait, along with the honeycomb.

Raspberry feuilletine

Makes one large 18cm square mould/tray.

Ingredients

For the nut biscuit

50g nut powder

50g sugar

5g cornflour

10ml honey

50g eggs

45g egg yolks

For the chocolate mousse

300g praline paste

150g feuilletine

75g white chocolate

For the raspberry jelly

250g raspberry purée

3g agar agar

For the chocolate glacage

250g dark chocolate (70%)

315ml double cream

150g sugar

65g cocoa powder

190ml water

For the raspberry sorbet

250g raspberry purée

125ml water

65g sugar

To garnish

Fresh Strawberries

Dark chocolate, melted

Method

For the nut biscuit.

Preheat the oven to 180°c. Whisk all the ingredients together until the mixture thickens. Spread on a baking tray and bake for 5 minutes.

Take a square or rectangle mould. Without overlapping any of the pieces of nut biscuit, cut to fit the mould.

For the chocolate mousse.

Melt the white chocolate. Warm the praline paste mix into the feuilletine and roll out between two pieces of parchment paper to ½cm thick, then freeze. Cut out to the exact shape of your mould and press this in nice and flat.

For the raspberry jelly.

At room temperature, whisk the agar agar into the raspberry purée and bring to the boil in a pan whilst continually whisking. Pour onto the feuilletine and freeze.

For the chocolate glacage.

Bring the sugar and water to the boil to create a sugar stock.

In a separate pan bring the double cream to the boil and whisk in the cocoa powder.

Pour over the chocolate and leave for 5 minutes to melt. Whisk again to create smooth ganache, then pour over the sugar stock and whisk everything together.

Take your frozen feuilletine out of the mould and pour over the glacage. Leave in the fridge to defrost until thawed. Portion and finish with fresh strawberries.

For the raspberry sorbet.

Bring the water and sugar to the boil then add in the purée and churn.

For decoration melt a piping bag of 70% chocolate and pipe a nice pattern.

Leave some of the purée to fill in the holes in the chocolate, just like the picture.

Lemon tart and blackcurrant ice cream

The simple beauty of a good lemon tart is difficult to top. This is a dish that requires technique, finesse, skill, time and patience. This is the first dish I ask all new WF recruits to make to see how they fair with something seemingly so simple. Serves 6.

Ingredients

For the pastry

145g plain flour

75g unsalted butter

25g ground almonds

50g icing sugar

1 egg

For the lemon topping

1 lemon, zest only

125ml lemon juice

375ml double cream

7 egg yolks

65g caster sugar

For the blackcurrant ice cream/ sorbet

700ml water

250g fructose

1kg blackcurrants, pureéd

60ml lemon juice

30ml vodka

Method

For the pastry.

Place everything except the egg in a blender and blitz until the mixture resembles breadcrumbs.

Add the egg and blitz to bind the mixture.

For the lemon topping.

Reduce the lemon juice with the zest to about half the original amount.

Add the cream to the lemon juice and bring to a boil. Leave to cool down to room temperature.

Lightly whisk the egg yolks and sugar and then add in the cream mixture.

For the blackcurrant ice cream/sorbet.

Heat the water and fructose in a pan until the fructose has fully dissolved.

Purée the blackcurrants, leave the pips in as it will be strained later.

Allow to cool until tepid, then whisk in the pureéd blackcurrants, lemon juice and vodka.

Strain through a sieve and cool over ice.

Transfer to an ice cream maker and churn until it reaches -5°c, alternatively place into a container in the freezer and whip up every hour to keep soft.

Store in the freezer until required.

To assemble the dish.

Roll out pastry to 1cm thick.

Line your chosen mould/tin with the pastry and trim to size.

Prick with a fork and then bake at 200°c for 2 minutes.

Egg wash the pastry and then bake again for 2 minutes until golden brown.

Top the pastry with the lemon filling and cook at 95°c for 1 hour.

Cool uncovered.

Serve immediately with a quenelle of blackcurrant ice cream/sorbet.

Don't *Panic*

"Why, sometimes I've believed as many as six impossible things before breakfast."

There's a tendency to panic and get stressed when confronted with a complex looking recipe, but it can all be avoided if a few golden rules are followed.

Firstly, remember the entire process is about enjoyment and it is meant to be fun. It's about learning, challenging yourself and experimenting with something new.

Secondly, planning is essential. The more you plan ahead and get involved with the process of sourcing ingredients, the more satisfying and hassle-free it will be.

I'm incredibly lucky with my lifestyle; I can create a carte blanche menu determined by what is growing in the field, which is immensely rewarding. To physically unearth an ingredient that is at its prime incites a wealth of inspiration, and has enabled me to create sophisticated dishes from humble beginnings. So if you can grow anything yourself, I urge you to do so. It will definitely get the creative juices flowing.

When you get back to the kitchen with your ingredients, try not to let the task ahead deter you. It's all about taking things step by step and working to your own level. Ask for help if necessary, and don't worry that things might take longer than they appear to – I have a whole team behind me, not many have a sous chef on hand at home…

Finally, cooking should be relaxing yet stimulating enough to create sense of jeopardy that plays with your emotions.

And if things really get too much, remember that a glass of red wine is the perfect way to lessen any feelings of anxiety you may have!

Breads

Onion bread

Makes 3 loaves.

Ingredients

750g strong white bread flour

20g salt

30g sugar

400ml water, at room temperature

80g dried onion flakes

50g fresh yeast

Oil, for greasing

Method

Roast the dried onion at 180°c for 2 minutes, or until golden. Then add all of the ingredients in a mixing bowl and mix using an electric whisk on a medium speed for 5 minutes. Then turn the speed up and mix for another 5 minutes. Leave to double in size at room temperature, knock the dough back, shape into 450g loaves and place into greased loaf tins. Prove until it has doubled in size again and bake at 210°c for 20 minutes. Remove from the tins and place back in the oven at 180°c for another 12 minutes. Leave for 10 minutes to cool before slicing.

Brown bread

Makes 3 loaves.

Ingredients

250g strong brown bread flour

500g strong white bread flour

20g salt

30g sugar

400ml beer, at room temperature

50g fresh yeast

Oil, for greasing

Method

Add all of the ingredients in a mixing bowl and mix using an electric whisk on a medium speed for 5 minutes. Then turn the speed up and mix for another 5 minutes. Leave to double in size at room temperature, knock the dough back, shape into 450g loaves and place into greased loaf tins. Prove until it has doubled in size again and bake at 210°c for 20 minutes. Remove from the tins and place back in the oven at 180°c for another 12 minutes. Leave for 10 minutes to cool before slicing.

Malt bread

Makes 20-25 buns.

Ingredients

1.5kg brown bread flour

1kg white bread flour

60g yeast

100g malt extract

50g salt

350ml water

150ml Guinness

150ml oil

450g treacle

Method

Preheat the oven to 200°c. Put all of the ingredients excluding the treacle into a mixing bowl. Using an electric mixer with the hook attachment mix for 10 minutes on speed 3. Add the treacle and portion into 45g rolls. Cover with cling film then leave to prove. Cook at 200°c for 10 minutes.

You can mix this by hand if you're feeling brave.

Bread sticks

Makes up to 50 breadsticks depending on thickness.

Ingredients

450g white bread flour

10g salt

10g sugar

90ml olive oil

20g yeast

170ml water

16ml squid ink

Method

Preheat the oven to 200°c. Mix all of the ingredients in an electric mixer with the hook attachment on a medium speed for 5 minutes. Roll into a pasta machine on thickness 4, or roll out with a rolling pin to about 2cm thickness. Using the roller cutter, make into long rectangle shapes and lay in a greased baking tray. Brush with oil and sprinkle with Maldon salt. Bake at 200°c for 5-7 minutes.